Financial Integration and Real Activity

STUDIES IN INTERNATIONAL TRADE POLICY

Studies in International Trade Policy includes works dealing with the theory, empirical analysis, political, economic, legal relations, and evaluations of international trade policies and institutions.

General Editor. Robert M. Stern

John H. Jackson and Edwin Vermulst, Editors. *Antidumping Law and Practice: A Comparative Study*

John Whalley, Editor. *Developing Countries and the Global Trading System.* Volumes 1 and 2

John Whalley, Coordinator. *The Uruguay Round and Beyond: The Final Report from the Ford Foundation Project on Developing Countries and the Global Trading System*

Jagdish Bhagwati and Hugh T. Patrick, Editors. *Aggressive Unilateralism: America's 301 Trade Policy and the World Trading System*

Alan V. Deardorff and Robert M. Stern. *Computational Analysis of Global Trading Arrangements*

Ulrich Kohli. *Technology, Duality, and Foreign Trade: The GNP Function Approach to Modeling Imports and Exports*

Stephen V. Marks and Keith E. Maskus, Editors. *The Economics and Politics of World Sugar Policies*

J. Michael Finger, Editor. *Antidumping: How It Works and Who Gets Hurt*

Horst Herbert and Ngo Van Long, Editors. *Trade, Welfare, and Economic Policies: Essays in Honor of Murray C. Kemp*

Robert M. Stern, Editor. *The Multilateral Trading System: Analysis and Options for Change*

David Schwartzman. *The Japanese Television Cartel: A Study Based on* Matsushita v. Zenith

Barry Eichengreen. *Reconstructing Europe's Trade and Payments: The European Payments Union*

Alan V. Deardorff and Robert M. Stern, Editors. *Analytical Perspectives and Negotiating Issues in the Global Trading System*

Edwin Vermulst, Paul Waer, and Jacques Bourgeois, Editors. *Rules of Origin in International Trade: A Comparative Study*

Alan V. Deardorff and Robert M. Stern, Editors. *The Stolper-Samuelson Theorem: A Golden Jubilee*

Kent Albert Jones. *Export Restraint and the New Protectionism: The Political Economy of Discriminatory Trade Restrictions*

Alan V. Deardorff, James A. Levinsohn, and Robert M. Stern, Editors. *New Directions in Trade Theory*

Robert Baldwin, Tain-Jy Chen, and Douglas Nelson. *Political Economy of U.S.–Taiwan Trade*

Danny M. Leipziger, Editor. *Lessons from East Asia*

Bernard M. Hoekman and Petros C. Mavroidis, Editors. *Law and Policy in Public Purchasing: The WTO Agreement on Government Procurement*

Tamim Bayoumi. *Financial Integration and Real Activity*

Financial Integration and Real Activity

Tamim Bayoumi

Ann Arbor
THE UNIVERSITY OF MICHIGAN PRESS

332.042
B36f

2000 1999 1998 1997   4 3 2 1

Library of Congress Cataloging-in-Publication Data

Bayoumi, Tamim.
    Financial integration and real activity / Tamim Bayoumi.
        p. cm.   (Studies in international trade policy)
    Includes bibliographical references and index.
    ISBN 0-472-10870-0 (cloth)
    1. Capital movements.   2. Monetary unions.   3. Saving and
investment.   I. Title.   II. Series.
    HG3891.B39   1997
    332'.042—dc21   97-18822
                                                          CIP

Printed by Bookcraft (Bath) Ltd, Midsomer Norton

STUDIES IN INTERNATIONAL TRADE POLICY

For Susan, my wife, and Phyllis, my mother

Contents

List of tables		*page* viii
List of figures		ix
Preface		xi
1	Introduction	1
	Capital mobility	
2	International capital mobility: an overview	11
3	Saving and investment correlations and international capital mobility	30
4	Consumption and international capital mobility	54
	Optimum currency areas	
5	The theory of optimum currency areas	77
6	Empirical work on optimum currency areas	95
7	Economic integration and optimum currency areas	118
8	Concluding observations	135
	Bibliography	141
	Index	153

Tables

3.1 Saving–investment regressions for 22 OECD
countries, 1960–93   *page* 32
3.2 OECD regressions across successive time periods,
1960–93   36
3.3 Time-series regressions using different definitions
of investment for selected OECD countries, 1961–86   39
3.4 Time-series correlations for Canadian provinces,
1962–93   40
3.5 Saving–investment regressions across Canadian provinces 43
3.6 Saving–investment regressions across different
time periods   44
4.1 Correlations of consumption and real GDP growth
across 21 OECD countries, 1973–90   58
4.2 Consumption regression across 21 OECD countries,
1973–90   61
4.3 Correlations of consumption and GDP growth across
the 10 Canadian provinces, 1972–93   67
4.4 Consumption correlations across the 10 Canadian
provinces, 1972–93   68
6.1 Correlations of estimated aggregate supply disturbances
in western Europe, 1963–90   98
6.2 Correlations of estimated aggregate supply disturbances
in the United States, 1963–86   99
6.3 The size of automatic stabilizers (percent offset to
a change in income)   105
6.4 Canadian provincial trade ratios, 1989 (percent of GDP) 107

Figures

2.1   Financial liberalization in Japan and the
      United Kingdom   *page* 16
3.1   Saving–investment ratios in 22 OECD countries
      over different time periods   37
3.2   Saving and investment ratios across regimes   46
7.1   The trade model   122

Preface

In a world of information overload, it is incumbent on authors to explain why they are providing another addition to the printing presses of the world. I had two main aims in writing this book. The first was to provide a survey of two areas of economics in which I have been involved – international capital mobility and optimum currency areas – which was both technically proficient and, at the same time, approachable. In this endeavor, I was assisted by the nature of the subjects chosen. Neither has attracted the mathematical formalism which is prevalent in many of areas of economics, and which makes much of the current work in these areas somewhat abstruse, at least for my taste. So, I have not had to make the choice between accuracy and approachability, but rather have been able to write a book which will be (I hope) useful for a relatively wide range of potential readers.

My second aim in surveying these two areas of international finance in a single volume was to underline their close connection. Capital mobility looks at the impact of the financial system on the real economy, while optimum currency areas looks at the impact of the real economy on the financial system. They are, thus, different sides of the same coin. Combining both subjects in a single work thus provides a holistic view of the interactions between the real side of the economy and the level of financial integration – hence the title of the book.

Any author requires a certain amount of support, and I am no exception. I would like to thank Mike Artis for first suggesting the topic, for giving me encouragement during the process of writing, and, most importantly, for giving useful comments on the draft as it slowly appeared. Linda Tesar, Holger Wolf, Peter Kenen, Paul Masson, and Ronnie MacDonald also gave helpful comments on parts of the text. Susanna Mursula and Jeff Gable provided research assistance. Special thanks go to my wife, Susan, who gave sympathy, support, advice and encouragement. Finally, many of the ideas presented here reflect the product of joint work with other economists. In addition to those already mentioned, my greatest debt by far is to Barry Eichengreen, who has given me constant inspiration and insight, without which this book would not have been written. Thanks to all.

1 Introduction

This book provides an overview of recent work on international capital mobility and optimum currency areas. Both topics have enjoyed something of an academic renaissance over the past few years, driven, as most such renaissances are, by events in the real world. Progress towards European Monetary Union (EMU), most importantly the Treaty on European Economic and Monetary Union (the Maastricht treaty) signed in February 1992, has brought a new immediacy to the need to assess the costs and benefits of a currency union. Additional impetus has been provided by the break-up of currency unions in eastern Europe and, most strikingly, in the former Soviet Union. Nor is the interest limited to Europe. It is entirely possible that free trade groupings in other parts of the world, such as the countries in the North America Free Trade Agreement (NAFTA), the Latin American Free Trade Association (LAFTA) in South America, and the Association of South-East Asian Nations (ASEAN) in Asia, will, like the European Union before them, produce moves toward a single currency.

At the same time, the problems of the Exchange Rate Mechanism (ERM) in Europe in 1992–93 illustrated the potential disadvantages of a close cousin of a currency union, namely relatively fixed exchange rates. In part, the problems of the ERM reflected the move to free capital mobility across participants. It was these capital markets which allowed the massive international capital flows which dislodged so many currencies from their chosen pegs.

Interest in international capital mobility is not limited to the problems of the ERM. The period since 1945 has seen a veritable revolution in international capital markets. Until the late 1960s most industrial countries severely restricted capital flows across countries through direct controls of one sort or another.[1] These controls have been gradually whittled away over time to the point where currently no important limitations on capital movements remain between

1

industrial countries. Interest in international capital mobility has also been stimulated by academic controversy. In 1980, at a time when most international economists believed capital mobility to be relatively high, Charles Horioka and Martin Feldstein published an article in which they argued that the observed behavior of saving and investment across countries indicated capital mobility to be very low (Feldstein and Horioka, 1980). This test remains controversial, and the solution to the 'Feldstein–Horioka' puzzle is still open to debate.

Whatever the final resolution to this discussion – and I will provide my own reading of the literature in Chapter 2 – the freeing of international capital markets is clearly one of the more important trends in the international economy over the last 30 years. By widening the range of options available, open capital markets improve the allocation of consumption, saving, and investment across countries. This liberalization is also, in many respects, very recent. Understanding the implications of this change therefore requires more than an analysis of time-series data since (say) 1970. It is also necessary to understand how this behavior has been affected by the change in financial markets which has occurred in the interim. Economic theory can help to furnish answers. So can analysis of other regimes with high capital mobility, such as the pre-1914 gold standard or comparisons of behavior between regions within a country. The latter illustrates another connection between capital markets and currency areas. Virtually all currency unions involve free capital movements within the monetary area.

International capital mobility and optimum currency areas are thus both topical issues. At first glance, however, they might appear to be strange bedfellows. One appraises the impact of different levels of access to capital. The other deals with the advisability of adopting a common currency, thereby fixing exchange rates and lowering the costs of doing business between the participating regions. To be sure, most currency unions involve free capital movements across participating regions. On reflection, however, these two issues have a more fundamental link. The literature on capital mobility, or at least the focus used in this book, looks at the implications of capital market integration for the behavior of real activities such as consumption and investment. Similarly, the literature on optimum currency areas focuses on the interaction between this underlying real behavior and the choice of currency regime.

The underlying theme of the book is thus the interaction between the financial system and the real economy. The first part of the book, on capital mobility, focuses on the impact of the financial regime on real activity. It explores how changes in capital mobility can affect investment, saving, and consumption. Reversing the causation, the second part of the book, on the theory of optimum currency areas, explores the impact of underlying real behavior on the choice of the monetary regime. It thus explores how the real side of the economy affects the level of financial integration. Reviewing both sides of the interaction between financial integration and the real economy allows a less partial view of the relationship between the financial regime and real activity than is usually the case (capital mobility and optimum currency areas are generally treated as separate and relatively distinct issues in international finance). My aim in reviewing the two literatures in one volume is to provide a more unified and holistic understanding of the interactions between the real economy and financial systems.

Before discussing the remainder of the book in more detail, it may be useful also to discuss what this book is not about. The focus is on macroeconomics. There is little discussion of the implications of policies for different industries or groups of people. At the other end of the scale, this book does not aspire to high theory. In particular, there is a movement in academic economics to assume that the world economy is close enough to perfection to be approximated by a model with perfectly flexible prices, full information, and complete markets ('real business cycle' theory). Such an approach provides little insight into either of the issues discussed here. The assumption of full information and complete markets implies that there is perfect capital mobility across countries. The issue of testing the actual level of capital mobility thus becomes essentially irrelevant. Similarly, the assumption of perfect price flexibility makes the exchange rate a redundant price, as any change in relative prices caused by the exchange rate can be achieved equally easily by an equi-proportionate change in all domestic prices. It is domestic price stickiness which makes the exchange rate a superior instrument for changing relative prices, and hence makes the choice of whether to join a currency union important. In short, those seeking a tract on the international aspects of 'real business cycle' theory should look elsewhere.

Chapter 2 provides an overview of the literature on capital mobility. As has already been noted, the period since the late 1960s has seen a major change in international capital market arrangements in industrial countries, which have gradually moved from having significant controls upon such transactions to no controls at all. Interest in international capital mobility has been further enhanced by the fact that alternative tests of the level of international mobility appear to provide strikingly different answers to the same questions. Tests which use comparisons of market prices between countries (in particular, nominal interest rates) to measure capital mobility indicate that international capital mobility is currently high. By contrast, tests which focus on the behavior of real activities, such as correlations between saving and investment or comparisons of national consumption paths, indicate that net capital flows between countries are significantly lower than would be expected if capital markets were very open.

A popular explanation for this difference in results is that the tests using real activity, which are based on the predictions of simple macroeconomic models, are misspecified, and that, properly adjusted, the results from these tests are consistent with high capital mobility. While accepting this as a possibility, I argue that a more convincing explanation for the dichotomy between the two types of tests is that they measure different concepts of capital mobility. Comparisons of market interest rates measure current access to international capital markets. Tests using macroeconomic quantities, by contrast, look at how far individuals use such markets to improve the intertemporal allocation of saving, investment, and consumption. To use capital markets in this way implies not only that individuals have access to capital markets currently, but that they believe that this access will continue in the future, and that this access is independent of actual outcomes. Hence, even if access to international capital markets is currently high, individuals' use of capital markets to smooth quantities intertemporally may be only partial if they remain uncertain about future access to such markets.

The subsequent two chapters then review two tests of capital mobility which focus on the behavior of real activity across countries. Chapter 3 considers the work on correlations of saving and investment ratios across countries initiated by Feldstein and Horioka's finding that such rates are highly correlated. The discussion differentiates between the high time-series correlations between saving and investment – which appear to be a characteristic of the business cycle, and have little to say about capital mobility – and the high but declining cross-sectional correlations across nations. The latter result appears to differ significantly from the behavior observed within countries (where capital mobility is known to be high and saving and investment are not correlated), implying that net capital flows are lower across countries than within them. Similarly, current correlations of saving and investment also appear to be larger than those observed during the heyday of the classical gold standard from 1880 to 1913, a period during which international capital mobility is believed to have been high. In addition, there is a decline in the observed cross-sectional correlation between saving and investment across industrial countries over the last 30 years which corresponds to the reduction in capital controls. In short, the evidence from natural experiments in which capital mobility is known to be high indicates that the Feldstein–Horioka test may indeed be a useful measure of capital mobility, where capital mobility is defined as the willingness of individuals to use capital markets to improve the intertemporal path of investment.

Chapter 4 looks at the evidence on capital market integration provided by international consumption patterns. The central insight behind this literature is the risk sharing hypothesis, namely that consumption patterns across individuals with access to capital markets (and, by analogy, countries with such access) should be very highly correlated with each other over time, and unrelated to individual circumstances and, in particular, changes in local income. Empirical evidence indicates, however, that consumption patterns across countries are not highly correlated with each other and are highly correlated with local conditions. A number of explanations for this finding are reviewed, and some new results using data on consumption across Canadian provinces are presented. I conclude that the most likely explanation for the lack of correlation of consumption paths across countries is the existence of higher transaction costs across national borders than within them, consistent with the continued existence of significant barriers to financial and real transactions between nations.

The next three chapters discuss the literature on optimum currency areas. Chapter 5 provides an overview of the theory of optimum currency areas, largely developed in the 1960s by Robert Mundell and others, which looks at the benefits and costs of adopting a single currency within an area. The focus of the literature then, as now, was on the underlying structural factors which alter the costs of losing monetary autonomy. These costs depend most fundamentally upon the size of asymmetric disturbances in activity, as it is such differences in performance which provide the main motivation for having an independent monetary policy, and hence a flexible exchange rate. In addition, there are a number of factors which can partially substitute for flexible monetary and exchange rate policies: wage and price flexibility, factor mobility, fiscal policy, and private capital markets. Other factors also impact the effectiveness of monetary and exchange rate policy to solve macroeconomic imbalances, including the diversity of sectoral production and openness of the economy. Differences in the preferences of policy makers and in the legal and financial structure of economies can also affect the desirability of forming a currency union. Finally, theoretical work is also progressing on the benefits of a single currency in terms of lower costs of transactions and a more stable unit of account.

Chapter 6 reviews the empirical work on optimum currency areas. While the theory was largely developed in the 1960s, the empirical counterpart to this work has mainly been developed since the late 1980s, as a result of progress toward monetary union in western Europe. Again, the focus has been very largely on the costs of losing monetary autonomy. Considerable progress has been made in many directions, such as identifying the size and symmetry of underlying disturbances, measuring the size of fiscal automatic stabilizers, and the role of private capital markets in reducing the impact of region-specific disturbances. In addition, earlier work on factor mobility, wage and price flexibility, and the diversity and nature of underlying disturbances has been incorporated and extended. The result is that we have a fairly good empirical understanding of most of the factors which determine the costs of forming an optimum currency area, although little progress has been made on integrating these divergent factors into a single estimate of overall costs. Like its theoretical counterpart, the empirical literature on the benefits of an optimum currency area is considerably less developed than that on the costs, although significant progress has still been made in this area.

Chapter 7 presents some original theoretical work on an area which has not been analyzed in any detail to date, namely the interaction between greater economic integration and optimum currency areas. As the example of western Europe illustrates, the interest in forming a currency union appears to be closely associated with moves toward economic integration, in particular in trade. An important issue is therefore how trade integration changes the desirability or lack of desirability of a currency union. The chapter presents a demand and supply framework, and uses it to discuss the merits of the very divergent analyses of this issue to be found in the existing literature.

The final chapter provides some concluding thoughts. The theory of optimum currency areas appears to provide a number of useful, and empirically implementable, guides as to which parts of the world might, or might not, benefit from a common currency. Unfortunately, however, this analysis has not progressed far enough to be able to make accurate estimates of the net value of a single currency for a particular region. While this reflects uncertainties in estimating both the benefits of a single money and its costs, the larger uncertainties are involved in the estimates of benefits. In addition, there is increasing evidence, both from the work on capital mobility discussed in this book and from comparisons of levels of trade and of goods prices, that countries are much less integrated with each other than they are internally. In short, national boundaries are still a significant impediment to economic integration.

Taken together, these conclusions point to a world in which there is a significant limit to the amount of integration which can be achieved without a common currency – or without, at a minimum, open international capital markets combined with a fixed exchange rate regime of the permanence and solidity of the classical gold standard. Given the notable fragility of post-1945 fixed exchange rate systems, particularly when combined with open international capital markets, this implies a relatively stark choice for national policy makers between adopting a common currency and high levels of economic integration with neighboring states or choosing to have separate currencies and a somewhat lower level of economic integration. In short, decisions about whether or not to participate in currency unions may well become an increasingly frequent policy decision in the twenty-first century.[2]

Notes

1 As a child in England, I vividly remember going to the bank where my mother had to have her passport stamped in order to collect our foreign currency for a vacation.
2 Eichengreen (1995) provides a similar analysis.

Capital mobility

2 International capital mobility: an overview

International capital markets provide the same benefits across countries that domestic capital markets provide within them. By connecting potential lenders and borrowers they lower the cost of financial transactions, thereby improving both the quality and quantity of saving and investment. They increase the efficiency of the capital stock by making the (risk-adjusted) cost of capital more equal across potential borrowers and raise consumer welfare by allowing a path that is nearer to optimal for consumption over time.

These benefits do not require that the participants in these markets are always correct. Borrowing and lending are, by their very nature, an uncertain business. As long as markets price these uncertainties correctly given existing information, they will improve economic welfare.[1] The benefits from open capital markets, both domestically and internationally, have been increasingly recognized over the last 20 years, which has been one factor in the worldwide trend toward financial deregulation and liberalization.[2]

The same period has seen considerable academic interest in measuring the level of capital mobility between countries. One reason for this interest is that it helps to assess the impact of financial deregulation on the international economy. Twenty years ago the majority of countries in the industrial world, particularly within Europe, imposed significant controls on capital transactions. Currently, by contrast, no significant capital controls remain.[3] Important steps along the way include the abolition of capital controls by the newly elected Thatcher government in the United Kingdom in 1979, the deregulation of international capital markets in Japan in the early 1980s, and the abolition of remaining capital controls within Europe (in particular in France and Italy) at the end of 1992 as part of the European Union's Single Market program. A parallel move toward deregulation of international financial markets has occurred in many developing countries, although in this case most countries still retain some controls.

The impact of this change on the levels of net flows of capital between countries is clear. In the 1950s and 1960s imbalances in current accounts were small and variable. As the current account is equal to the negative of the capital account, the size of net international capital flows was also lower. Economies were essentially constrained to provide for their consumption and investment out of domestic resources. By contrast, the 1980s and 1990s have seen a significant increase in both the size and the persistence of current account imbalances, and hence capital flows, between nations.[4]

These developments represent only the latest in a series of historical changes in the nature of international capital markets. During the nineteenth century, and in particular in the time of the pre-1914 gold standard, such markets were almost completely free of government controls. The efficiency of the underlying financial markets is illustrated by the tight constraints on movements in exchange rates imposed by nineteenth-century international capital markets. Private capital markets limited the fluctuations in exchange rates around their implied parities (defined by the commitment to convert each currency into a fixed amount of gold) to a narrow band similar in size to those found in modern financial markets, with the width of the band being defined by the costs of transporting gold between countries (the 'gold points').[5] The result was a world in which there were large and persistent net capital flows between countries.[6]

International capital markets failed to operate as smoothly in the interwar years. The huge size of, and uncertainties in, international payments for reparations and outstanding loans after the First World War created significant strains early in the period. The great depression in the 1930s, and the coincident rise in tariffs and decline in trade in goods, exacerbated these problems and led to a number of defaults on international loans which, in turn, hurt the world economy.[7]

With this experience in mind, the architects of the postwar international economic system who met at Bretton Woods in New Hampshire in 1944 focused on reviving international trade in goods, but put little importance on the need to provide open international capital markets. In particular, the Articles of Agreement of the newly formed International Monetary Fund, set up to oversee the international financial system, required signatories to aim to eliminate exchange controls on current international transactions but allowed countries to retain controls on capital transactions. As a result, the period up to the collapse of the Bretton Woods exchange rate system in 1973 was one of very limited capital flows. The revival of international capital markets during the 1980s and 1990s, therefore, represents a deviation away from the system that prevailed during the immediate post-1945 period, and back toward that which was in place prior to 1914.

Clearly, international capital markets have been significantly liberalized over the last 20 years. What remains unclear, however, is the current level of international capital mobility. Have international markets been integrated to such an extent that capital flows as freely and easily between nations as within them, and individuals can borrow and lend internationally with the same ease that they can do within their own country? Or is international capital market integration more limited, so that significant inefficiencies still exist in the allocation of consumption, saving, and investment across countries? These are the questions which the literature on international capital mobility aims to answer.

Interest in international capital mobility has been further enhanced by the fact that alternative tests of the level of such mobility appear to provide strikingly different answers to these questions. These tests can be divided into two broad categories. One category uses comparisons of market prices (such as nominal interest rates) to measure capital mobility, while the other uses the behavior of real activities (such as the behavior of saving and investment) to the same purpose. Broadly speaking, tests which use nominal interest rates, such as those which compare the rate of return on assets denominated in the same currency but issued in different places, indicate that international capital mobility is currently very high. By contrast, tests which focus on real activities, such as correlations between saving and investment or comparisons of national consumption paths, indicate that net capital flows between countries are significantly lower than would be expected if capital markets were very open – at least using relatively simple models of behavior.

Microeconomic tests of capital mobility

The logic behind using comparisons of nominal interest rates to measure capital mobility is that, in the absence of restrictions on movements of capital, securities with the same characteristics should yield the same rate of return. The price of a given US federal government security is the same whether it is bought in New York or Los Angeles, as is the return on a UK government security in London and Glasgow. The reason for this is that transportation costs for securities are essentially zero – all that is needed is for some relatively simple information to be exchanged between the buyer and seller – so that the usual costs which can cause the price of physical goods to vary between locations do not apply. Accordingly, the only major reason for interest rates to vary across locations is existing or prospective government regulations on capital flows.[8] As there is no realistic probability of differential regulations being imposed within countries, interest rates on nationally traded securities are basically identical nationwide.

The problem with doing such comparisons across different countries is that it is difficult to find securities with identical characteristics. For example, attempts to compare (say) pound sterling interest rates in London with French franc rates in Paris on otherwise identical assets is complicated by the fact that any such comparison requires one to make assumptions about the future path of the exchange rate. As, in the absence of a currency union, the future path of the exchange rate is inherently uncertain, it is necessary to decide whether differences in interest rates reflect government regulation or market expectations about the future path of exchange rates.

There has been a considerable literature on the relationship between exchange rates and interest rates.[9] The results indicate that interest rates on highly traded short-term instruments in Euro-markets predict the value of that currency in the appropriate futures markets well. More general tests of market efficiency, looking at the relationship between interest rate differentials and actual future exchange rates, have been less successful. However, the observed deviations are rarely attributed to low capital mobility, but rather are generally thought to reflect failures of other maintained hypotheses, such as risk aversion or the symmetry of expectations.

A more direct approach used by researchers to look at capital mobility is to compare interest rates on securities denominated in a single currency but traded in different countries, the so-called 'onshore–offshore' interest rate differential. Hence, for example, a comparison is made between the rate of interest charged on 90-day US dollar loans in New York to the rates charged on 90-day eurodollar loans in London. If these rates coincide, at least after adjustment for the costs of transactions, then capital markets are considered to be highly integrated. If there are large unexplained differences between onshore and offshore interest rates, then the presumption is that these differences reflect capital controls, which limit interaction between the two markets.

Numerous comparisons of this type have been made.[10] The results show clear evidence that capital controls did lead to significant differences in onshore–offshore interest rates in the past. They also show that these differences have essentially disappeared across industrial (although not all developing) countries, indicating that international capital markets are currently very highly integrated. In many cases these changes are dramatic. Figure 2.1, for example, shows the change in the onshore–offshore interest rate differential in the United Kingdom and Japan both before and after the abolition of exchange rate controls. Prior to deregulation, onshore–offshore interest rate differentials were often as large as 2 or 3 percentage points. After deregulation, the differential between the two rates has remained small even in the face of considerable movements in the absolute level of interest rates.

The evidence from onshore–offshore interest rate differentials appears strongly to support the idea that capital mobility, at least across a limited number of highly traded assets, is by now very high, spurred by a general move to reduce capital account restrictions.[11] Such evidence is also supported by the enormous turnover in foreign exchange markets (which now comprise the largest financial market in the world) and rising cross-border holdings of assets.[12]

At the same time some discrepancies remain. In particular, despite recent increases in cross-border holdings of assets, portfolios still appear much less internationally diversified that might be expected. Even in a world with few capital controls to prevent individuals from holding assets of other countries, investors appear to have a strong bias to domestic assets. Put another way, investors do not seem to not use access to international markets to insure against country-specific disturbances as theory would lead us to expect.[13] One would also expect high capital mobility to produce a close connection between real interest rates across countries. However, empirical tests generally reject real interest rate parity.[14] The dichotomy between the acceptance of (covered) nominal interest rate parity and the rejection of real interest rate parity is presumably connected with the failure of

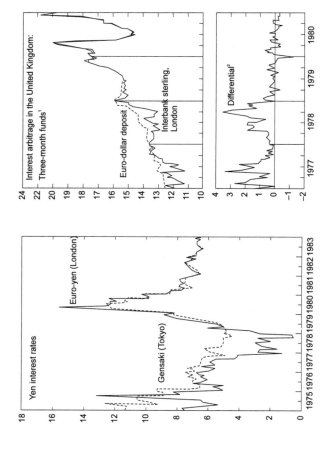

Figure 2.1 Financial liberalization in Japan and the United Kingdom: the impact on the offshore–onshore differential (annual percentage).

[1]Averages for week ending Wednesday.
[2]Positive differentials favor dollar assets.
Source: Artis and Bayoumi (1990).

purchasing power parity (PPP) to explain short-term movements in nominal exchange rates. If movements in price levels across countries are not closely connected to movements in their bilateral exchange rates, then there is no strong reason to expect a close correspondence between the behavior of real and nominal interest rates.

Macroeconomic tests of capital mobility

Up to this point the discussion has focused upon tests of whether individuals have access to international capital markets. Onshore–offshore interest rate comparisons inform us that domestic and foreign financial markets are closely connected. They do not, however, tell us very much about whether individuals are actually using international capital markets to improve their welfare. An alternative approach to measuring capital mobility tests how far actual outcomes correspond to what might be expected if individuals use such capital markets beneficially. In theory such tests could be carried out at any level of analysis, including data on individual firms or households. In practice, however, these tests have generally been macroeconomic, looking at whether net capital flows into or out of countries correspond to what might be expected given the paths of variables such as national output, investment, saving, and consumption. For this reason, I will refer to this approach as the *macroeconomic* approach to capital mobility, in contrast to the *microeconomic* approach just discussed, which looks at access to markets and is epitomized by onshore–offshore interest rate comparisons.

The most widely used of these macroeconomic tests involves looking at the correlation of saving and investment. This test, which was introduced in Feldstein and Horioka (1980), involves regressing saving rates on investment rates across countries. To understand the logic behind the test, consider a world with an integrated capital market and a single world real interest rate. As capital markets are integrated, saving from any particular country can be thought of as going into a global pool, while investment in different countries comes out of this pool, implying that decisions to save and to invest in any particular country are separated from each other. Accordingly, there is no particular reason why countries with high saving ratios should also have high investment ratios.

By contrast, if international capital mobility is low, so that the amount that countries can contribute to or take out of the global pool of saving is limited, countries will be forced to finance investment mainly from domestic saving. Indeed, in the extreme case of no capital mobility, when the analysis is that of a closed economy, domestic saving and investment rates will be equal by definition. Hence, high correlations between rates of saving and investment across countries is consistent with low international capital mobility. An alternative way of looking at this test is to recall that the difference between saving and investment is the current account. If saving and investment are highly correlated this implies that current account imbalances, and hence capital flows between countries, are small in comparison with international differences in saving and investment.

Feldstein and Horioka found that the coefficient on a cross-sectional regression of saving rates on investment rates across a sample of industrial countries was very close to (and insignificantly different from) one. This, they concluded, was evidence of low capital mobility. Subsequent investigators using the saving–investment test have consistently found that saving and investment are highly correlated across countries. As the next chapter discusses this literature in detail, my observations at this point will be limited to generalities.

The first is that most investigators, with the notable exception of Feldstein, have tended to argue that this does not necessarily mean that there is low international capital mobility. The essence of their arguments is that the assumption underlying the test, that saving and investment should not be correlated in the presence of high capital mobility, need not be true. Both saving and investment are highly endogenous variables, and one can construct models with high capital mobility where saving and investment move in tandem in response to various types of shock. However, empirical evidence from situations in which capital is known to be highly mobile (discussed in the next chapter) seem to indicate that the implicit assumption behind the test does indeed hold, and that saving and investment rates are largely uncorrelated in situations of high capital mobility.

A second observation is that these saving–investment correlations appear to have fallen over the last 20–30 years. Investigators who have looked at the correlation of saving with investment across countries over successive time periods have generally concluded that these coefficients were lower in the 1980s than in the 1970s, and that in the 1970s they were again lower than in the 1960s.[15] Hence, the saving–investment regressions appear to be capturing some increase in international capital mobility since the 1960s, coincident with a period over which controls on international financial transactions have been falling.

This suggests that the saving–investment tests may be more useful than is generally acknowledged. Looking back over time, it now appears clear that international capital mobility was low over the 1960s and early 1970s, the period covered by the original test by Feldstein and Horioka, although many at the time felt capital was relatively mobile. It is not impossible that a similar process, in which people believe capital to be highly mobile although on reflection it may turn out not to be, is occurring currently. The continuing high correlation between saving and investment may indeed be indicating that net flows of capital between countries are abnormally small.

The second macroeconomic test of capital mobility, discussed in more detail in Chapter 4, involves looking at the implications of the desire to smooth consumption on capital flows. This can be done either by looking at the path of consumption directly or by looking at the implied path for the countries' external balances, the latter approach being generally referred to as the intertemporal approach to the current account.[16] In either case, the basic point is that if consumers have open access to a global capital market and a single world real interest rate, then utility maximization has implications for the path of consumption and of external balances across countries.

The advantage of this approach is that its theoretical underpinnings are much stronger than those for correlations of saving and investment. The disadvantage is that there is considerable evidence that individuals do not fully smooth consumption even within a country.[17] As capital markets within countries are free and open, this implies that there are other impediments to smoothing consumption, such as the desire to save for a rainy day (the 'precautionary saving motive') or an inability to borrow ('liquidity constraints'). Hence, the failure to find consumption smoothing across countries could reflect either low capital market integration or other factors which limit the degree of such smoothing even within countries. These issues are taken up again in Chapter 4.

Bearing this caveat in mind, the bulk of the empirical evidence on consumption smoothing indicates that net capital flows across countries are considerably smaller than would be expected if capital markets were fully open, at least when considering relatively simple models of consumption.[18] It also indicates that capital markets have been becoming more open over time.[19] Thus, the general evidence from saving–investment correlations and from consumption-based tests are in accord. Both approaches tend to reject the notion that international capital markets have enabled countries to follow the best path over time, while finding a trend toward improved allocation of resources over the last two or three decades.

Reconciling the difference in results

The results from macroeconomic tests, that net capital flows across countries are smaller than might be expected, contrast strongly with those from microeconomic tests, which generally indicate that access to capital markets is high. A popular explanation for this dichotomy is to argue that capital mobility is indeed high and that the macroeconomic tests are flawed because one or other of the auxiliary assumptions that are required in the derivation of the models do not hold.[20] In the case of saving–investment correlations this explanation generally centers around the existence of common shocks which cause saving and investment to be correlated within a country, even when capital is fully mobile.[21] For consumption smoothing these explanations include differences in real interest rates across countries caused by the failure of PPP, imperfections in the use of domestic capital markets, and the existence of nontraded goods.[22]

There is no doubt that the macroeconomic tests do involve unrealistic assumptions, as do most economic models. However, the existence of these imperfections does not necessarily imply that the results from such tests are wrong. This is particularly true when the deviations from the idealized path are large and highly significant, as they are in the case of the macroeconomic tests. In addition, as discussed in the next two chapters, there is by now considerable empirical evidence as to the behavior of saving, investment, consumption, and the current account in environments in which capital markets are clearly free and open, such as behavior across different geographic regions within a country. These comparisons point to a significant difference between behavior across countries and that within them, a supposition which supports the notion that net capital flows between countries are indeed abnormally low.

An alternative explanation for the differences between the two types of tests is that both sets of results are correct, and that there is difference between the *types* of 'capital mobility' being tested. The microeconomic tests look at whether certain arbitrage equations involving short-term instruments hold. Hence, they look at the existence of *current* access to capital markets. They have nothing to say about whether or not this access is expected to continue into the future, at least beyond the maturity of the short-term securities (generally 6 months or less) used in the calculations. By contrast, the macroeconomic tests look at whether net capital flows are being used to improve the path of the economy over time. Hence, the very essence of these tests is that capital markets are not only open now, but are expected to remain open in the future, and that this access is independent of the behavior of international capital flows and the concomitant flows of goods and services.

This difference in the nature of the propositions being tested provides a potential explanation for the observed empirical dichotomy. Access to international capital markets may well be currently extremely high, as illustrated by the close connection between onshore interest rates and their offshore equivalents. However, this does not in itself mean that individuals will use the markets to improve the path of the economy over time if they perceive a possibility that these markets will not remain fully accessible in the future. To take an extreme example, suppose that capital markets were open in a country this year, but that it was known with certainty that they would be completely closed from next year on. In these circumstances interest rates on domestic 3-month Treasury bills would still move in tandem with their offshore counterparts, but few would use capital markets (say) to smooth consumption over the cycle.

Is it reasonable to assume that individuals do not believe that future access to international capital markets is a foregone conclusion? Such an assumption does not appear particularly outlandish. Several smaller European countries were prepared to reimpose capital controls during the European exchange rate turmoil in 1992–93, and it is difficult to believe that other countries in the region did not at least consider this option. More generally, even countries of the size and importance of the United States are not fully insulated from such pressures. The appreciation of the US dollar in the mid-1980s provoked significant domestic protectionist sentiment. This pressure was seen in calls to limit foreign access to US markets for both goods and assets. On the goods side, the harm caused to the manufacturing sector by the high level of the dollar caused serious debate on the need to protect 'the rust belt' from competition. Similarly, Japanese acquisition of various well known US assets, such as the Rockefeller Center, generated calls to limit foreign access to certain types of investment.

Such sentiments reflect a range of political forces. However, in the case of the United States in the mid-1980s the most important impetus was clearly the problems that the appreciation of the exchange rate posed for the manufacturing sector. Any capital inflow has to be matched by an equal deficit on the current account. The counterpart to the large inflows of capital in the mid-1980s was an appreciation of the exchange rate, a widening of the current account deficit, and a shift in production from traded to nontraded goods. If such a shift in resources could be done without cost, this might not create significant political pressures. However, the reality is that firms go out of business and workers get laid off.[23] In short, the capital inflows of the 1980s caused significant costs to some very specific sectors of the economy. In a representative democracy this will almost inevitably lead to significant pressures to limit these costs, which in turn implies reducing the size of capital flows.

The example of the United States in the mid-1980s also illustrates the possibility that continuing access to capital markets may be conditional on the outcomes they generate. As long as the current and capital accounts remain within certain boundaries, political pressures will likewise be limited. If these markets, however, create sufficient domestic economic disruption then this will create political pressures to limit this harm. In short, the behavior of market traders may well be limited by political constraints. As long as these constraints are understood by market participants themselves, they will avoid breaching these limits as doing so would generate financial losses through the lost turnover caused by government regulations. Simple self-preservation will limit behavior. Although the comparison is by no means exact, there is some similarity to the target zone literature, in which the knowledge that governments are prepared to limit exchange rate fluctuations generates expectations which by themselves keep market-determined exchange rates within the target zone.[24] In this case, however, it is the threat of government actions which causes outcomes to be constrained.

To provide a simple and very hypothetical example to do with political constraints, let us suppose that in the absence of political pressures the current account deficit of the United States would be 4 percent of gross domestic product (GDP) and the analogous surplus of

Japan would be 6 percent of its GDP, a not unreasonable assumption given the wide difference in saving rates between the two countries. It is difficult to believe that, if these outcomes were actually realized, over a short span of time there would not be overwhelming political pressure to limit this imbalance. As a result, while the observed US current account deficits and Japanese surpluses reflect the underlying pressures to transfer capital from Japan to the United States, these deficits may well be significantly smaller than those which would occur in the absence of these countervailing political forces.[25]

Devaluations can also cause political conflict, although this mainly occurs in developing countries. This presumably reflects the fact that consumption of imported goods in these countries is often heavily skewed towards specific groups in society, whether it be modern consumer goods for the middle class or imported basic food stuffs for the poor. Depreciated exchange rates generally cause less political pressure in industrial countries, possibly because the costs of such a devaluation, in the form of higher prices for imported goods, are borne relatively evenly across different groups in the economy. The overall lesson would appear to be that general sacrifice is an easier pill to swallow politically than costs which cover a more limited section of the community.

It is not, in fact, necessary to look at the interests of different groups in society in order to generate political economy arguments as to why flows of goods between countries might be lower than those that would be predicted in a fully competitive world. Another factor is the existence of sovereign immunity. Such immunity makes it difficult to sue national governments over their actions, thereby making it easier for a country to default on international loans. Obstfeld and Rogoff (1996, Chapter 6) discuss a number of ways in which the combination of sovereign immunity and moral hazard may tend to reduce the level of international capital flows. Such problems are less pervasive within countries as the national legal system is generally better defined, thereby reducing the scope for reneging on future obligations.

Another reason why capital flows between countries could be constrained is that governments have an incentive to manipulate the terms of trade in their favor by using tariffs. The appendix to this chapter presents such a model, which is an intertemporal version of the optimum tariff argument. In this example, countries produce goods in different periods. Trade is therefore beneficial as it allows individuals in these countries to smooth consumption over time. However, each country has an incentive to put a tariff on exports to the other country. The reason is that, in the absence of retaliation, the gains to welfare from the extra income created by a tariff outweigh the losses to welfare from the resulting distortion of relative prices, at least initially. Such a tariff will also, however, generally reduce net trade, as it raises the cost of goods which have been exported from one country to the other. Here, then, is another mechanism through which net trade, and therefore flows of capital between countries, could be limited by the actions of national governments.

Finally, the costs of trading have to be factored into any calculation of the benefits of open capital markets. Transaction costs and uncertainties of changing currencies may well tend to reduce some potential trades between countries, although the size and efficiency of the underlying markets are such that this may well be a secondary consideration.

Conclusions

Arguments of this type, whether to do with political economy constraints, sovereign immunity and moral hazard, optimum tariffs, or transaction costs, all imply that the ability of capital markets to provide the desired path for consumption and investment over time may well be constrained across countries in a manner which is unlikely to occur within them. In such a situation tests of intertemporal smoothing will find that observed capital flows will correspond only partially to those implied if markets operated without constraints. It also provides an explanation of the home bias of many investors. If international capital markets retain significant uncertainties, they are less useful as a way of smoothing behavior over time. Hence, this mechanism provides an explanation for several observed facts of modern international capital markets. Such considerations are less likely to constrain domestic capital markets as data on net capital flows are difficult to obtain and the imposition of capital controls is very difficult.

It is instructive to contrast the current situation with that which prevailed during the last period of open international capital markets and large net capital flows, namely the classical gold standard that existed between 1880 and 1913.[26] Compared with the current day, there were a number of factors in this earlier period which tended to reduce the political pressures generated by capital flows.[27] One factor was the limited understanding of the relationship between government actions and the economy, which reduced the impulse to call on the government to intervene in the operations of markets. Another was the limited political power of those most affected by international competition. Labor movements were in their infancy, and the vote was (with the important exception of the United States) generally limited to men of property. In addition, for many peripheral members of the international community, there was the very real threat of direct military intervention – otherwise known as gunboat diplomacy. Finally, the nominal exchange rates of the core members of the system were remarkably stable over the period. There were no changes in gold parities (the rate at which currencies were convertible into gold) for any of the core countries between 1880 and 1913, and hence changes in real exchange rates occurred relatively slowly. All of these meant that capital flows in the pre-1914 regime may well have been less liable to generate political pressures.

The political economy of that period was, however, very different from that of the current day. Increased belief in the ability of governments to control the economy together with representative democracy make it unlikely that governments will wish to renounce entirely the possibility of intervening in international commerce in goods and assets when they are perceived to be hurting significant parts of the electorate, or are thought not to be in the interests of the economy as a whole. Indeed, one of the great strengths of democratic systems is that they respond to the wishes of the populace. Such responsiveness, however, may put constraints on the ability of individuals to use capital markets to improve their own welfare over time. In this sense, international capital flows may remain limited for some time to come.

True integration of capital markets across regions may require a mechanism which makes the charting of external imbalances extremely difficult, thereby reducing political pressures to 'do something' about them. Monetary unions generally have this characteristic, as it is difficult to measure accurately transactions between regions within such a union and it is a complex matter to control capital movements even if one so desires. Such an approach puts a new light on the interest within Europe of boosting regional economic integration through the creation of a single currency.

Appendix: a simple intertemporal optimum tariff model

This appendix constructs a simple model in which governments have an incentive to follow policies which will lower net trade. Consider a world made up of two periods and two countries. In the first period the single consumer/worker in country A produces 2 units of the single tradeable good and country B has no production. In the second period the single consumer/worker in country B produces 2 units of the good, and country A produces nothing. Trade between the two countries is costless. Finally, it is assumed that neither country is able to buy equity in the production of the other country because of moral hazard problems.

Each country has a single representative consumer with a time-separable utility function of the form:[28]

$$U(c_1, c_2) = (c_1^{1-\sigma} + c_2^{1-\sigma})/(1-\sigma) \qquad (2.1)$$

The price of goods in country A in period 1 is set equal to 1 as the numeraire, while the price of goods in period 2 in country B is p_2. In the case where no tariffs are levied, these will also be the prices of the goods in the country which is not producing in that period, as trade itself is costless. In this case, the solution to the problem is:

$$c_1^A = c_1^B = c_2^A = c_2^B = p_2 = 1 \qquad (2.2)$$

In the first period, country A exports 1 unit of the good to country B, and receives 1 unit back in period 2. Hence, consumption smoothing creates large net flows of goods in both periods, from country A to B in the first period, and from B to A in the second.

Consider, now, the solution if the government in country A is able to impose a tariff (t) on exports to B in the first period, but that it is assumed that B does not impose a tariff in period 2. In this case, the price of goods in the first period is 1 in country A but $1+t$ in country B. Similarly, the income of country A is no longer 2 (its output of the good in period 1 multiplied by the price of the good in period 1), but:

$$y^A = 2 + t(2 - c_1^A) \qquad (2.3)$$

The solution to this problem is:

$$c_1^A = \frac{1 + t}{1 + t + p_2^{1+\sigma}} \qquad c_1^B = \frac{(p_2/t)}{1 + (p_2/t)^{1+\sigma}}$$

$$c_2^A = \frac{(1 + t)p_2^{\sigma}}{1 + t + p_2^{1+\sigma}} \qquad c_2^B = \frac{(p_2/t)^{1+\sigma}}{1 + (p_2/t)^{1+\sigma}}$$

(2.4)

There is an implied relationship between t and p_2 defined by the resource constraint in period 1 ($c_1^A + c_1^B = 2$), but the equation has no closed-form solution. Accordingly, it is not possible to calculate a general formula for the optimum tariff level.

One can, however, prove that a very small tariff raises welfare in country A. An increase in the tariff from zero to ε, where ε is very small, raises consumption in country A as follows:

$$\Delta c_1^A = \varepsilon(1-\sigma)/4$$

(2.5)

$$\Delta c_2^A = \varepsilon(1+\sigma)/4$$

As the levels of consumption of the two goods are (to a first approximation) still equal, so are their marginal utilities. It follows that utility must rise for country A, and fall for country B. One can also show that the optimum tariff is not infinite, as an infinite tariff produces autarky, which provides a lower level of utility than the case when no tariff is imposed.

What happens to the trade balance? As long a $\sigma < 1$, that is, the intertemporal rate of substitution is below 1 – a fairly general assumption – consumption of the good in country A in period 1 rises as the tariff rises, implying that trade with country B falls. Hence, the trade balance generally falls in the period in which the tariff is imposed.

In the case when both countries are able to impose tariffs, the logical solution is that both countries charge infinite tariffs, and that net trade is zero. To see this, note that in period 2 country B has no incentive to trade as it can always do better by keeping the goods for itself, which it can do by imposing an infinite tariff. Given that this is the optimum strategy of country B, it follows that country A has no incentive to trade in the first period, so it will also impose an infinite tariff. It should be stressed that this very stark outcome reflects the simplicity of the model, and in particular the fact that country A produces nothing in the second period. The general point, however, that governments have an incentive to impose tariffs which lower net trade, appears general. Whichever country is producing the most in any period has the larger market power, and hence an incentive to impose a larger tariff than the other country. Hence, net trade is likely to be reduced even in more general models than that presented here.

Notes

1 A caveat to this is the 'law of second best'. If the rest of the economy contains inefficiencies, then a move to greater efficiency in one area need not improve overall welfare.
2 Documented in Mussa *et al.* (1994).
3 Mussa and Goldstein (1993). Details of restrictions on international transactions across a broad range of countries can be found in *Exchange Arrangements and Exchange Restrictions*, an annual publication by the International Monetary Fund.
4 Artis and Bayoumi (1990).
5 Hallwood *et al.* (1996) and Giovannini (1993). The introduction of the telegraph was the main factor behind this high level of efficiency. The telegraph cable connecting the United States to the United Kingdom cut the time for settling transatlantic financial transactions from three weeks to one day (Irwin, 1996), making it, in many respects, a more profound change in the operation of financial markets than the computer.
6 Bayoumi (1990).
7 Fishlow (1985).
8 Tax liabilities can, and on occasion do, vary by location. For example, some US state bonds are free of home state taxes. This creates a higher demand for such bonds from home state tax payers than from others. However, as these bonds can still be sold anywhere, the prices of such bonds are the same in all locations.
9 See Taylor (1995) for a survey.
10 For example Frankel (1993).
11 The removal of capital restrictions across countries is discussed in some detail by Goldstein *et al.* (1993).
12 Group of Ten (1993).
13 Mussa *et al.* (1994) and Tesar (1995). Some of this lack of diversification may reflect the recentness of the move to open capital markets. It is very possible that portfolios will become highly diversified over the next 10–20 years. However, currency risk, lack of availability of information, and the weakness of international law may continue to create a home bias.
14 Edison and Pauls (1993) and Cumby and Mishkin (1986). Gagnon and Unferth (1993), however, conclude that real interest rate parity holds across a number of countries with open capital markets, with the important exception of the United States.

15 See, for example, the regressions in Bayoumi (1990) or Feldstein and Bacchetta (1991). More evidence on this point is presented in the next chapter.

16 Examples of consumption tests include Obstfeld (1994) and Lewis (1996a). An early exposition of the intertemporal approach to the balance of payments is contained in Sachs (1981), while Obstfeld and Rogoff (1994) give a review.

17 Browning and Lusardi (1996) provide a survey of the microeconomic literature on consumption.

18 Obstfeld (1995) and Tesar (1995) give surveys.

19 Obstfeld (1995).

20 See the reviews of the literature by Frankel (1993) and Obstfeld (1995). A more general explanation for this dichotomy could also be that capital markets have been fully liberalized only relatively recently and that most tests use data from periods in which it is generally believed that capital mobility was limited.

21 Obstfeld (1986) and Tesar (1991).

22 For example Lewis (1996a).

23 Such costs also have to be borne in mind in evaluating the benefits of open international capital markets.

24 Krugman (1991c).

25 This has many similarities with an explanation of why net capital flows between countries may be small which is often treated separately, namely that governments target their current account position (Fieleke, 1982; Summers, 1988; Bayoumi, 1990). This explanation has fallen somewhat out of favor in the absence of any reasons as to why they might do this. The argument in the text provides a political economy reason as to why governments might want to limit the size of current account imbalances. I refer to it as a limitation on capital mobility rather than a function of government policy because, unlike a current account target which has been chosen as a macroeconomic target by the government, such forces appear more fundamental and less arbitrary.

26 Between 1880 and 1913 the average current account surplus of the United Kingdom was 4.5 percent of gross national product (Bayoumi, 1990).

27 Similar arguments are made in Eichengreen (1995, Chapter 4).

28 The subjective discount factor has not been included as it has no significant impact on the analysis.

3 Saving and investment correlations and international capital mobility

Most literatures in economics are gradual affairs in which recent work progresses steadily from earlier endeavors. The work focusing on the correlation between saving and investment, however, is an exception to this rule. Prior to the article by Feldstein and Horioka published in 1980 nobody had even thought about using the relationship between saving and investment across countries as a way of measuring the level of international capital mobility. Subsequently, all work on this topic has had to face the 'Feldstein–Horioka puzzle.'[1]

Feldstein and Horioka (1980) argued that, in a world with high capital mobility, an increase in the global pool of saving caused by an increase in the domestic saving rate will produce an increase in investment in all countries, with the increase in investment in each country 'vary[ing] positively with each country's initial capital stock and inversely with the elasticity of the country's marginal product of capital schedule.' The generalized nature of the increase in investment implies a low regression coefficient of domestic saving on domestic investment. A high coefficient, by contrast, would imply that most of the incremental saving in a country remained there, in turn implying constraints on the ability of saving to move between countries. An important caveat to the test, which was acknowledged in the paper, is that a high coefficient on saving could reflect common causes of variation in both domestic saving and investment. Feldstein and Horioka went on to argue, however, that a large coefficient on saving would be strong evidence against high international capital mobility, and 'would place on the defenders of that hypothesis the burden of identifying such common causal factors.'

Their test of capital mobility was therefore to run a regression of ratios of saving on investment.[2] More specifically, their estimating equation was:

30

$$(I/Y)_i = \alpha + \beta \,(S/Y)_i + \varepsilon_i \qquad (3.1)$$

where $(S/Y)_i$ is national saving as a ratio to GDP (averaged over several years), $(I/Y)_i$ is the equivalent ratio for investment, and ε is an error term. This is the most uncomplicated type of regression it is possible to estimate, involving, as it does, a single independent variable and a constant term.[3] The simplicity of the estimating equation, however, does not imply that the implementation was not sophisticated. Indeed, the real strength of the paper is the care with which the estimation was accomplished.

The basic result that Feldstein and Horioka found was that using data across 16 members of the Organization for Economic Cooperation and Development (OECD) for 1960–74, the coefficient on saving in the above regression was large, insignificantly different from one, and very highly significantly different from zero.[4] Along the way, they dealt comprehensively with the major econometric issues raised by such a regression. For example, while their main focus was on the results using gross saving and investment, they also estimated the equation using net values for both series. They tested for the adequacy of the linear formulation by including a quadratic term in saving in the regression. They investigated the impact of including the rate of growth of population and real GDP in the specification, and whether the coefficient on saving varied with openness of the economy to trade or the size of the economy. They used instrumental variables such as demographic ratios, the benefit–earnings replacement ratio, and the growth in private income to investigate the potentially important issue of simultaneity bias caused by common causal factors. Finally, the relationship between medium-term changes in saving and investment was investigated, as well as the relationship between levels of saving and investment. None of these concerns significantly affected the basic results.

A measure of their success in regard to the econometric issues involved in the estimation is that few subsequent authors have questioned their results in terms of statistical technique.[5] Numerous subsequent researchers have confirmed the existence of a high correlation between saving and investment across countries, to the point where it is now a 'stylized fact' about the international economy.[6] To illustrate these results, Table 3.1 reports the results from two cross-sectional regressions of national saving on investment for 22 OECD countries over 1960–74 and 1975–93.[7] The 1960–74 results are very

Table 3.1   Saving–investment regressions for 22 OECD countries, 1960–93

Time period	Coefficient on saving
1960–74	0.84 (0.07)**
1975–93	0.65 (0.10)**

Regression: $(I/Y)_i = \alpha + \beta(S/Y)_i + \varepsilon_i$
The estimated constant terms are not reported. Standard errors are reported in parenthesis.
**Significant from zero at the 1 percent level.

similar to those found by Feldstein and Horioka using the same sample period, namely that saving and investment are highly correlated and close to one (although at 0.84 the point estimate on the coefficient on saving is slightly lower than the one they report, and is significantly different from unity at the 5 percent level, but not at the 1 percent level). The estimated coefficient for the more recent 1975–93 period is 0.65, still very different from zero, but now also clearly significantly different from one, suggesting a diminution in the correlation over time – an issue which will be discussed further below.[8]

The high correlation between saving and investment identified by Feldstein and Horioka for industrial countries led them to conclude that capital was not very mobile between countries. In order to explain how this could be true despite the existence of significant day-to-day international capital transactions between banks, they argued that only a small part of the world capital stock was held in liquid form suitable to eliminate short-term interest rate differentials, while most capital is unavailable for arbitrage activity since it is in long-term investments. Such a distinction, however, ignores the possibility that capital within a country is fungible, and that many international transactions involve direct claims on real capital, such as real estate or equities.

Such potential weaknesses in the explanation for their results may be one reason why most observers have rejected the article's conclusion that international capital mobility is limited. In the absence of a good reason as to why differing types of capital should have different levels of mobility, most authors have assumed that all capital must be as mobile as that between major international banks. The previous chapter put forward some views as to why net flows of capital between countries might be small even when capital flows freely between major banks, and why this could be legitimately defined as low capital mobility, defined as the ability to use capital markets to improve intertemporal paths of saving, investment, and consumption over time. Such an argument provides a potential reconciliation of the observation that capital flows freely between major banks with the central observation of the Feldstein and Horioka paper, namely that net capital flows across countries are small compared with saving and investment rates.

Other work using international data

The next major contribution to the literature was a paper by Maurice Obstfeld, published in the *Carnegie–Rochester Conference Series* in 1986. Obstfeld's main contribution was to look more carefully at the theoretical background to the assumption that saving and investment would be uncorrelated in a world of high capital mobility. In essence, the paper can be seen as a demonstration that the common causes downplayed by Feldstein and Horioka in their original discussion could, indeed, generate the kind of correlations between saving and investment found in the data.

The issue can be best seen by considering the underlying determinants of both saving and investment:

$$(I/Y)_i = \beta\, X_i - \phi\, R_i + \varepsilon_{Ii}$$

$$(S/Y)_i = \delta\, Z_i + \gamma\, R_i + \varepsilon_{Si}$$

(3.2)

where X and Z are vectors of independent variables determining investment and saving across countries, respectively, R_i is international real interest rate, and the εs are error terms. Feldstein and Horioka argued that if capital markets are open, and hence real interest rates are the same across countries, there is no reason for saving and investment to be correlated. In a situation of low capital mobility, however, the inability of capital to flow internationally will cause national real interest rates to differ in such a manner as to make saving and investment ratios within a country similar and net capital flows small. The 'common cause' explanation of the saving–investment correlations, by contrast, notes that if the explanatory variables for investment and saving, X_i and Z_i, both contain the same variables (for example, demographic trends) then saving and investment can be correlated even when real interest rates are equal across countries.

Obstfeld constructed just such an example. He created an over-lapping generations model in which saving and investment across countries are highly correlated even in the presence of high capital mobility due to differential rates of growth of population. The model assumes that individuals live for 2 periods, working when young and retiring in old age. As they smooth consumption over time, individuals save in their youth and run these assets down in old age. Perfect capital mobility implies that individuals in different countries face the same real interest rates, and hence the saving rate of each generation is the same across all economies. Accordingly, the aggregate saving rate in any economy depends upon the relative size of the young and old generations, with economies with a higher rate of growth of the population having larger relative numbers of the young, and hence higher saving rates. On the production side, the (internationally immobile) labor of the young is combined with capital to produce goods, with high capital mobility again ensuring that the marginal return to capital, and hence the capital–labor ratio, is the same across economies. Economies with a higher rate of growth of population, and hence of the labor force, accordingly also require a higher rate of growth of the capital stock, and therefore more investment. A simple calibration of the model using data from actual economies indicated that this mechanism could produce a correlation between saving and investment that was similar to that found by Feldstein and Horioka.

Obstfeld's paper contains a second model in which saving and investment are highly correlated, but in this case the focus is on relationships over time rather than across countries. In this example, an economy with a representative consumer who lives forever faces a favorable technology shock which dies down gradually over time. The higher productivity results in a significant boost to investment, as the marginal product of capital rises. At the same time, the increase in wages temporarily increases earnings above their long-term level, which leads to an increase in saving through consumption smoothing. Again, the result is a correlation between saving and investment. Finally, at the end of this example Obstfeld goes on to discuss other mechanisms which are not included in the model which could generate further correlations between these two variables.

Obstfeld thus accepted the theoretical challenge laid down by Feldstein and Horioka when they said that common causes were unlikely to be the reason for the close observed correlation between saving and investment. The paper demonstrated that it was indeed possible to generate reasonable theoretical models which could yield correlations of the type observed in the data. Similar counter-examples have been generated subsequently by a number of other authors, partly reflecting the increased interest in 'equilibrium modeling' produced by the literature on real business cycles. Indeed, replicating a high (time-series) correlation between saving and investment became one of the stylized facts by which such 'equilibrium' theoretical models have come to be judged. Tesar (1991) provides a survey of earlier contributions to this literature. More recent work includes that of Baxter and Crucini (1993), who focus upon the effects of productivity disturbances in a two-country real business cycle model.[9] Baxter and Crucini also provide citations to a number of other papers in which high correlations between saving and investment have been found in models in which capital is fully mobile.

This literature on equilibrium explanations for the correlation of saving and investment, however, contains several potential weaknesses. The most obvious is that providing mechanisms by which an equilibrium model with high capital mobility is able to replicate observed correlations between saving and investment is very different from showing that the observed correlations are actually due to these mechanisms. All this work can essentially be seen as theoretical counter-examples to the original Feldstein–Horioka hypothesis that common causes were not empirically relevant. However, as will be discussed in detail below, the cross-sectional empirical evidence from situations in which capital mobility is almost certainly very high, such as within countries or during the pre-1914 gold standard, indicates that the saving–investment correlations are indeed low when capital mobility is high. Hence, empirically, the Feldstein and Horioka null hypothesis appears to be confirmed, at least as regards cross-sectional regressions.

A second concern with this literature is that it cannot explain why the cross-sectional relationship between saving and investment has apparently changed over time. Recall that the coefficient on saving in a regression using data from 1975–93 was considerably smaller than the equivalent value over 1960–74 (Table 3.1). When the period is divided more finely, a clear downward trend in the coefficient on

Table 3.2 OECD regressions across successive time periods, 1960–93

Time period	Coefficient on saving
1960–69	0.86 (0.06)**
1970–79	0.77 (0.11)**
1980–89	0.63 (0.10)**
1990–93	0.61 (0.09)**
Change between 1960–69 and 1990–93	-0.25 (0.11)*

Regression: $(I/Y)_i = \alpha + \beta(S/Y)_i + \varepsilon_i$
The estimated constant terms are not reported. Standard errors are reported in parenthesis.
*Significant at the 5 percent level.
**Significant at the 1 percent level.

saving can be identified. This can be seen in Table 3.2, which gives the coefficient estimates on saving–investment regressions using data from 22 OECD countries for four successive subperiods between 1960 and 1993. From 1960–69 to 1990–93 the coefficient on saving falls, from 0.86 to 0.61. As can be seen from the results at the bottom of Table 3.2, this fall of 0.25 in the coefficient on saving has an associated standard error of 0.11, implying that the fall is statistically significant at the 5 percent level.[10]

Figure 3.1 illustrates the underlying data. It shows the associated scatter plots of saving–investment ratios over these successive time periods. There is a clear change in behavior over time, with the relationship between saving and investment becoming flatter and slightly less well defined. It appears that something has occurred over time to alter the cross-sectional relationship between saving and investment across developed economies. Equilibrium models fail to provide an obvious explanation for such a change in behavior of saving and investment across countries over different time periods.

A third concern with this literature involves distinguishing between time-series and cross-sectional relationships. Recall that the original Feldstein–Horioka result referred specifically to a cross-sectional regression using data averaged over several years in order to abstract the relationship from any cyclical effects. Their justification for not presenting time-series evidence was that the data might well be

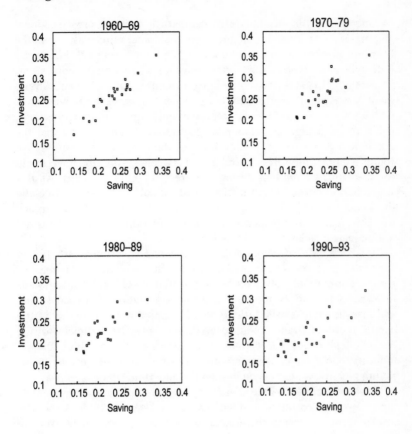

Figure 3.1 Saving–investment ratios in 22 OECD countries over different time periods

dominated by the common causes which generate business cycles. Except for the original 'overlapping generations' argument by Obstfeld, all the theoretical demonstrations of high correlations between saving and investment have focused on cyclical behavior, exactly the type of behavior which the cross-sectional regressions were designed to eliminate.

One reason for this failure to distinguish between cross-sectional and time-series behavior in the theoretical literature was a parallel blurring in the empirical literature. While the original article by Feldstein and Horioka reported only cross-sectional regressions, Feldstein's (1983) follow-up included evidence that saving and investment were highly correlated both across countries and over time, while Obstfeld (1986), who reported only time-series regressions, again found a high correlation in postwar data, and argued that the coefficient depended on the openness of the economy.[11] Obstfeld also found a high time-series correlation between saving and investment for the United Kingdom during the pre-1914 gold standard. As this was a period during which international capital markets were free and the United Kingdom was the dominant economic power, he argued that this was further evidence that saving–investment correlations did not indicate a lack of capital mobility.

It is certainly of interest that saving and investment are highly correlated both across time and across countries. However, the reasons for the correlations may well be very different. There are many ways that the economic cycle could generate correlations between saving and investment that have little to do with capital mobility. Even a little capital mobility (trade credit, reserves, etc.) may be sufficient to ride out cyclical needs for capital. On the obverse side, high capital mobility could be consistent with a positive cyclical correlation of saving and investment depending on the underlying shocks.[12]

Cyclical factors do indeed appear to be an important component of the time-series correlation of saving and investment. Table 3.3 shows results from regressing the annual change in the investment ratio on the change in the saving ratio for a number of different countries (the results were originally reported by Bayoumi, 1990). The first column shows the results when total investment is used as the dependent variable. All countries except Norway (which went through an oil boom) have a positive correlation between saving and total investment. In the second column the results from the same regression are reported, but using fixed investment instead of total investment as the dependent variable. This change in the definition of investment, which takes out inventory investment, lowers the observed correlation between saving and investment in every case. As changes in inventories are clearly driven by cyclical factors, this would appear to be strong evidence that the causes of the time-series correlation between saving and investment may well be largely cyclical.

Table 3.3   Time-series regressions using different definitions of investment for selected OECD countries, 1961–86

	Total investment		Fixed investment		Difference in coefficients
United States	1.00	(0.10)**	0.49	(0.07)**	-0.51
Japan[a]	0.84	(0.15)**	0.55	(0.11)**	-0.29
Germany	0.87	(0.17)**	0.32	(0.16)*	-0.55
United Kingdom	0.33	(0.18)	-0.02	(0.10)	-0.35
France	0.80	(0.26)**	0.19	(0.13)	-0.61
Canada	0.83	(0.16)**	0.25	(0.13)*	-0.58
Norway[a]	-0.21	(0.31)	-0.55	(0.27)*	-0.34
Belgium	0.63	(0.12)**	0.41	(0.09)**	-0.22
Finland	0.98	(0.30)**	0.10	(0.19)	-0.88
Greece	0.73	(0.13)**	0.40	(0.12)**	-0.33

Regression: $\Delta(I/Y)_t = \alpha + \beta \ \Delta(S/Y)_t + \varepsilon_t$
Source: Bayoumi (1990).
The table reports estimates of β. Standard errors are shown in parenthesis.
[a]1966–86.
*Significant at the 5 percent level.
**Significant at the 1 percent level.

Further evidence in this regard can be found in Table 3.4, which repeats these regressions using annual saving and investment data for the 10 Canadian provinces.[13] Being part of the Canadian currency union, these provinces clearly operate in an environment of high capital mobility. The results for the 6 largest provinces (the provinces are listed in terms of size of GDP, with Ontario being the largest and Prince Edward Island the smallest), however, are very similar to those across countries. Total saving and total investment are highly correlated for all but one of these provinces, the exception being Alberta, which, like Norway, went through an oil boom over the period. These coefficients also fall significantly when fixed investment is used in place of total investment, again exactly like the results using national data.

The data for the four smallest provinces, however, fail to produce high correlations between saving and any definition of investment. This

Table 3.4   Time-series correlations for Canadian provinces, 1962–93

	Total investment		Fixed investment		Differ-ence in coeffi-cients	GDP in 1993 ($bil-lion)
Ontario	0.85	(0.15)**	0.32	(0.11)**	-0.53	286.8
Quebec	0.66	(0.24)**	0.29	(0.17)	-0.37	160.8
British Columbia	0.75	(0.20)**	0.38	(0.21)	-0.37	92.1
Alberta	-0.01	(0.15)	-0.04	(0.13)	-0.03	78.1
Manitoba	0.72	(0.24)**	0.02	(0.14)	-0.70	24.0
Saskatchewan	0.76	(0.21)**	-0.22	(0.09)*	-0.98	22.0
Nova Scotia	0.14	(0.12)	0.08	(0.10)	-0.06	18.0
New Brunswick	-0.28	(0.16)	-0.05	(0.11)	0.23	14.7
Newfoundland	-0.03	(0.26)	-0.09	(0.22)	-0.06	9.4
Prince Edward Island	0.20	(0.16)	0.14	(0.12)	-0.06	2.3

Regression: $\Delta (I/Y)_t = \alpha + \beta \Delta (S/Y)_t + \varepsilon_t$
Standard errors are reported in parenthesis.
*Significant at the 5 percent level.
**Significant at the 1 percent level.

could reflect their small size, as hypothesized by Obstfeld using national data. However, these provinces are also very highly dependent upon government grants (as will be discussed below, average total saving ratios over the entire estimation period are very low or even negative for these provinces owing to very large amounts of federal government dissaving).

Subsidiary regressions (not reported for the sake of brevity) indicate that the coefficient on regressions using private saving and private investment are larger than those using total saving and investment. Further evidence against the idea that the results reflect economic size comes from the results for Manitoba and Saskatchewan, the smallest of the six larger provinces, with high correlations between saving and investment. These two provinces, which are much less dependent on government grants, show positive time-series correlations between saving and total investment even though they are both less than one-tenth of the economic size of the Ontario, the largest Canadian province in terms of output. The impact of economic size on the correlations therefore remains unclear.

To summarize, in all probability time-series correlations between saving and investment have little to say about levels of international capital mobility. Rather, these correlations reflect behavior over the business cycle.[14] This brings us back to the original problem posed by Feldstein and Horioka, namely why, when averaged over the cycle, are saving and investment ratios so closely correlated or, to put it in another way, why are net capital flows between countries so much smaller than variations in saving and investment ratios?

Theoretical models containing this characteristic can be produced, as Obstfeld demonstrated. However, it also appears that theoretical models can be constructed in which the correlation is negative. For example, take an overlapping generations model with stable populations in each country, where individuals live for two periods and work twice as hard when younger than when older, but where the long-term rate of productivity growth varies between countries.[15] Investment will clearly be positively related to productivity growth, but saving will be negatively related as those in countries with high productivity growth anticipate their future prosperity by consuming more and saving less when they are young. Hence, in this model saving and investment would appear likely to be negatively correlated.

Results from environments of high capital mobility

Given such potential theoretical ambiguity, the best way to solve the actual relationship between saving and investment in an environment of high capital mobility would appear to be through empirical tests. An early attempt was provided in a paper by Murphy (1984). He looked at correlations between saving and investment across 143 large US corporations. As capital markets in the United States are well developed, and most large corporations have relatively easy access to them, he reasoned that the correlation across corporations would be a useful benchmark for underlying behavior in an environment of high capital mobility. His results indicated that saving and investment across corporations were highly correlated, and hence he concluded that the results reported by Feldstein and Horioka were consistent with a high level of capital mobility.

Other regressions using data on total saving and investment from regions within countries – which are also environments of high capital mobility – have, however, generated the opposite result. There are now several papers which look empirically at the correlation of saving and investment across regions within a country, including Sinn (1992) for the United States, Bayoumi and Rose (1993) for the United Kingdom, Thomas (1993) for Canada, Germany, and the United Kingdom, and Dekle (1995) for Japan.

The most comprehensive paper, in terms of the underlying data, is that by Dekle, who used data on 47 Japanese prefectures in his analysis. He found a significant negative correlation between total saving and total investment, the opposite of the result found across countries. This negative relationship appears to reflect the effect of government saving and investment. Rich prefectures tend to pay a higher proportion of their income in taxes than poor ones, while government investment tends to be a higher ratio of income in poorer regions than in richer ones. Hence, government saving and investment are negatively correlated. However, Dekle found that *private* saving and *private* investment were uncorrelated across prefectures. Very similar results are reported by Thomas, who also found that private saving and private investment were uncorrelated across regions in three countries, and that government behavior can generate a negative correlation between total saving and investment. Finally, the papers by Sinn and Bayoumi and Rose report no significant correlation using total saving and total investment.

To get a flavor of these regional results, Table 3.5 reports the results from some cross-sectional regressions that use total gross saving–investment ratios across the 10 Canadian provinces from 1961 to 1993.[16] For the full sample the coefficient on saving is extremely small (-0.07) and insignificant; total saving and total investment are uncorrelated across provinces. Looking at the data, however, it is also clear that government policies are important determinants of the underlying data. In particular, the total saving rates in the four small provinces located on the eastern seaboard were either very small or negative, reflecting the high level of federal dissaving in these provinces caused by federal equalization grants.[17] To adjust for this exceptional activity, federal government saving was taken out of the total saving rate, resulting in much more equal saving rates across provinces. The adjusted saving data yields a larger estimated coefficient (0.25), but it remains statistically insignificant at conventional levels.

These results illustrate the two basic conclusions of the existing literature on saving and investment across regions within countries. Government policies can affect the relationship between total saving

Table 3.5   Saving–investment regressions across Canadian provinces

	Full sample	Excluding federal saving
Coefficient on saving	-0.07 (0.08)	0.25 (0.30)

Regression $(I/Y)_i = \alpha + \beta(S/Y)_i + \varepsilon_i$
The constant terms are not reported. Standard errors are reported in parenthesis.

and total investment, but private saving and private investment across regions within countries are not significantly correlated. The latter result is the more important as it provides support for the assumption made by Feldstein and Horioka in their original paper that saving and investment ratios should not be correlated with each other when capital mobility is high. It is also relatively easy, on reflection, to explain why Murphy found a high correlation between saving and investment across US corporations. For a corporation, high saving rates (i.e. profits) indicate a high rate of return on capital. It is therefore not surprising that elevated rates of saving are closely correlated with high investment rates, as higher returns on capital can be expected to spur more investment in that field. The potential bias due to common factors is thus particularly potent for the corporate rates of saving and investment used by Murphy.

Regional behavior within a country represents one way of looking at what saving and investment correlations might be in an environment of high capital mobility. An alternative is to consider earlier historical periods in which international capital mobility is considered to have been very high. The pre-1914 gold standard provides an obvious choice in this respect. Unlike the interwar and post-1945 periods, the pre-1914 period had very few controls on the movement of capital between countries. In addition, the economic system operated relatively smoothly throughout the period, free from such post-1914 economic disruption as world wars, reparations, and the great depression.[18]

Bayoumi (1990) provided some initial evidence on cross-sectional saving–investment correlation during the pre-1914 gold standard, finding that there was little correlation between saving and investment between 1880 and 1913 using a sample of eight countries. The coefficient on saving over the full sample period was 0.29, with a standard error

Table 3.6   Saving–investment regressions across different time periods

	Pre-1914 gold standard (1885–1913)		Early 1990s (1990–93)	
	Full sample	*Excluding United States*	*Full sample*	*Excluding Japan*
Coefficient on	0.53	0.11	0.61**	0.53**
saving	(0.29)	(0.48)	(0.09)	(0.11)
R^2	0.25	0.01	0.69	0.55

Regression: $(I/Y)_i = \alpha + \beta(S/Y)_i + \varepsilon_i$
Data from Jones and Obstfeldt (1994), and Table 6.2.
Standard errors are reported in parenthesis.
**Significant at the 1 percent level.

of 0.46. The lack of a significant correlation between saving and investment reflected the large and persistent current account surpluses and deficits run by individual countries over the period.[19] An important caveat to these results, however, was the omission of the United States from the data set. Saving–investment ratios were significantly higher in the United States than in any of the other leading economies over this period (in many respects similar to the position of Japan since 1960). Adding the United States to the data set increases the correlation between saving and investment to the point where the coefficient on saving can become marginally statistically significant.[20]

There are also some measurement issues associated with the underlying data reflecting the multiple roles of gold as both a commodity and a means of payment. Jones and Obstfeld (1994) discuss these issues in some detail, and report saving and investment data on 12 countries for the pre-1914 gold standard period, including the United States. They also present regressions in which the coefficient on saving is positive and marginally significant, as found by Eichengreen. Table 3.6 shows some regression results I have obtained using the Jones and Obstfeld data. The first regression shows the results for the full sample of countries from 1885 to 1913.[21] The coefficient on saving is 0.53 and not quite significant at conventional levels. The point estimate of the saving coefficient is thus not dissimilar to the coefficient of 0.61 found using OECD data from 1990–93 (also reported in Table 3.6); however, the standard error on the gold standard coefficient is over three times as large as the equivalent estimate for the early 1990s. Clearly, the statistical evidence of a positive correlation is much stronger for the 1990–93 period than for the gold standard period. A further difference between the two data sets is in the importance of a single country with exceptionally high saving and investment for the results. In the case of the gold standard data, the elimination of the US data produces a dramatic reduction in the regression coefficient on saving, from 0.53 to 0.11. By contrast, the exclusion of the Japanese data from the more recent results produces a much milder reduction in the estimated coefficient, which continues to be highly significantly different from zero.

These results indicate a qualitative difference in the behavior of saving and investment across countries in the pre-1914 gold standard compared with more recent experience, regardless of whether the gold standard coefficient on saving is significant at the 5 percent level when the United States is included (as found by Eichengreen, Jones and Obstfeld) or not (as in Table 3.6). Of course, a similar general result, that saving and investment are not highly correlated in situations in which capital mobility is known to have been high, was discovered when comparing saving and investment behavior across regions within a country.

Figure 3.2 illustrates these differences graphically. It shows a scatter plot of the cross-sectional relationship between saving and investment across Canadian provinces,[22] countries during the pre-1914 gold standard, and countries in the early 1990s. (These are the underlying data behind the regression results reported in Tables 3.5 and 3.6.) Both the Canadian and the gold standard data show very wide variations between saving and investment ratios across regions or countries. By contrast, the data for 1990–93 indicate a relatively tight relationship between these two variables. These clear differences in behavior make it very difficult to accept the idea that recent behavior across countries simply reflects a natural tendency for saving and investment to be highly correlated even when capital mobility is high. Equilibrium factors such as productivity shocks or population growth would be expected to operate as forcefully across countries in the nineteenth century or across regions within a country as they do across economies today. The close correlation of saving and investment rates in 1990–93 thus remains an anomaly.

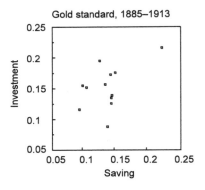

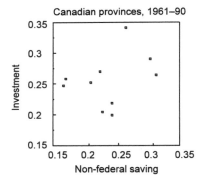

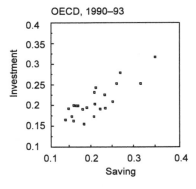

Figure 3.2   Saving and investment ratios across regimes

Interpreting the results

These results do not necessarily mean that the correlation between saving and investment reflects low international capital mobility. They do, however, imply that any explanation of the correlation over the recent period must be based on factors or shocks which are different currently than they were in the 1880–1913 period, or between regions within a country nowadays. Two such differences (in addition to low capital mobility) spring to mind. The first is exchange rate stability. The rate of exchange between the currencies of the major economic powers during the gold standard period was fixed by the convertibility with gold. As none of the major powers changed the parity with respect to gold between 1880 and 1913, bilateral exchange rates were both stable and anticipated to remain stable. Similarly, the rate of exchange across different regions within a country is fixed by the existence of a common currency. By contrast, exchange rates between different countries are currently highly variable, regularly changing by several percentage points within a month.

This variability in exchange rates has several implications. One is that the relative prices of goods across countries deviate from PPP, which, in turn, implies that expected real interest rates across countries can also vary. Frankel (1993) suggested that this variability could be a source of positive correlations between saving and investment, but without providing a mechanism by which such deviations in real interest rates would systematically increase the correlation between saving and investment. It should be recalled that the correlation between saving and investment in a world with low capital mobility is generated by differences in real interest rates across countries. Any argument based upon the existence of differences in real interest rates would therefore have to explain why this behavior might not be caused by low capital mobility.

Exchange rate variability may also generate uncertainty about returns on investment. If, as many have argued, exchange rates exhibit excess volatility (i.e. they vary more than can be justified by fundamentals) then the extra risk implied by such volatility could be sufficient to dampen demand for foreign assets. It is certainly true that most investors appear to have a significant home bias as regards their assets. At the same time, however, gross holdings of foreign assets have been expanding very fast over the last decade or so.[23] With the foreign exchange market now estimated to be the largest financial market in the world in terms of turnover, it appears difficult to believe that net flows of capital between countries is limited by a general disinclination to participate in such transactions.

A second difference between present behavior across countries and the situation during the gold standard or between regions within a country concerns the role of government policies. The work on saving and investment ratios within countries has already shown that government policy can affect the correlation between total saving and investment. Several authors, including Summers (1988) and Bayoumi (1990), have suggested that fiscal policies could have been used as a way of targeting the current account. According to this view, saving and investment are highly correlated with each other because governments have manipulated their accounts in order to achieve approximate external balance.

Formal tests of this proposition are complicated by the fact that merely observing that government saving and investment largely offset private imbalances is not sufficient to indicate that this behavior reflects conscious government policy. In a world of low capital mobility, these balances will also automatically tend to offset each other, although the causation presumably runs in the other direction, with changes in the government fiscal balance producing offsetting changes in net private saving through domestic real interest rates. To get around this problem, Artis and Bayoumi (1990) estimated government policy reaction functions for both fiscal and monetary policy. In both cases, the policy variable was linked to domestic factors, such as growth and inflation, and to the level of the current account balance. The results for fiscal policy showed little evidence that it had been actively used by governments to respond to current account imbalances. A more positive result, however, was found for the monetary policy reaction functions, where there was some evidence that interest rates had been used to move the current account back toward balance. On reflection, the negative result with respect to fiscal policy is hardly surprising given the complexity and length of the budgetary process in most countries. Fiscal policy is generally set only once a year in a highly political environment, making it difficult to imagine it being used successfully to achieve a specific current account target. By contrast, the relatively flexible and less overtly political channel of monetary policy is a more obvious instrument to achieve such a target.

There has been little recent work on government targeting of the current account, in part because of significant and persistent current account imbalances. These have made it appear a much less plausible that governments are trying to achieve a small external balance than it did even a decade ago. However, such considerations are a reminder of the speed at which such views have changed. While current account targeting may now be viewed by most economists as an oddity, it is not long ago that many economists (particularly in policy institutions) would not have regarded it as outlandish. It also means that much of the data used to test various hypotheses may come from periods when current account balance was regarded as a legitimate target for policy.

A further reason for taking theories about the role of government policies seriously is that even if policy makers no longer regard approximate current account balance as an objective, this does not mean that governments are indifferent about the external balance. The heated debate in policy circles over the 'Lawson doctrine,' the idea put forward by Nigel Lawson (then Chancellor of the Exchequer for the United Kingdom) in the early 1990s that current account imbalances caused by private markets were a matter of indifference to governments, illustrates the point. Most governments are not indifferent to the path of the current account (or to the level of the exchange rate, which helps to determine the current account).

This is a version of the argument put forward in the last chapter as the probable reason for the continuing correlation of saving and investment across countries. It essentially says that in a world in which governments seek to control macroeconomic outcomes, there may well be significant constraints on the sizes of net capital flows, although such constraints may be enforced through implicit rather than explicit rules. Such controls clearly do not operate within an economy. Apart from anything else, there is no record of capital flows, and hence control would be next to impossible. A similar lack of concern about capital flows is evident before 1914, when there was little faith in the ability of governments to improve overall outcomes by manipulating macroeconomic policies,[24] and external accounts were not generally calculated.

At the same time, the cross-sectional regressions across countries since 1960 do indicate that the deregulation of international capital markets over the last 20 years has gone some way to allowing capital to flow between countries. The fall in the slope of the relationship – as illustrated in Figure 3.1 and by the regression coefficients in Table 3.2 – indicates that capital has started flowing from countries, such as

Japan, which have high saving rates to low savers, such as the United States and United Kingdom. However, this process has not gone nearly as far as it could do, as is illustrated by the evidence from the pre-1914 gold standard.

It remains unclear whether the trend will continue or not. On the one hand, it is very possible that open capital markets will become so important to the world economy that governments will become less concerned about net flows of capital, and the observed correlation between saving and investment will continue to dwindle. An alternative view is that governments will continue to be concerned about external imbalances across countries and net flows of capital will continue to look small by the standards of the underlying differences in saving rates. Such an approach implies that the constraints on capital movements across countries are structural, in the sense that they are unlikely to be changed in the future. In either case, it is clear that changes in correlations of saving and investment over time will continue to be a useful barometer of the ability of individuals to use international capital markets to generate an improved international allocation of saving, investment, and consumption over time.

Conclusions

All this suggests a healthy future for work on saving–investment correlations. The time-series correlations should be accepted as a feature of the international business cycle rather than as a test of international capital mobility, as indeed appears to be occurring. Work on the cross-sectional results will continue to be of interest. One extension here could be to look at results across different regions of the world.[25] Another would be to see if adjusting saving rates in developing countries to reflect the flows of official financing produces the expected increase in saving–investment correlations across such countries. A third would be to look at government behavior with respect to the external position more closely. On the theoretical side, more work could be carried out looking at private sector behavior in worlds in which governments limit outcomes to those which are deemed to be in the interests of the country as a whole.[26] Exploring behavior in such models with 'political' constraints provides an exciting new direction for theorists.

Notes

1 Language is often an indicator of underlying attitudes. Saving–investment correlations across countries are generally called either a 'puzzle' or a 'paradox.' I suspect that these are not words which would have occurred to Feldstein and Horioka, who felt that the correlation reflected the existence of low international capital mobility. By contrast, the current usage implicitly assumes that the observed correlation is in some way aberrant from what might be expected, presumably because international capital mobility is actually high.

2 The simplicity of the regression also explains the slight oddity that a literature based on *regression* results is called one of saving–investment *correlations*.

3 Part of the reason for this simplicity is the cross-sectional nature of the regression. Many time-series issues, such as the correlation of the error term between periods or the importance of lagged independent variables, generally do not arise in this cross-sectional context.

4 For the full 1960–74 period the coefficient on saving was 0.887 with a standard error of 0.074 (using ordinary least squares).

5 Exceptions are Sinn (1992) and Taylor (1994). Sinn argues that annual data should be used rather than period averages as there is a tendency for current accounts to revert to zero over time. He found that annual data produce somewhat lower coefficient estimates than decade averages; however, the differences are not large. Annual averages confound long-term differences in behavior and cyclical effects, and may well increase measurement errors to the extent that the response of saving and investment to the cycle is different from its long-term behavior. I therefore continue to prefer five-year averages. Taylor argues that the simultaneity problems are so severe that saving and investment ratios should first be regressed on exogenous variables and then the residuals from the two regressions should be regressed on each other. This procedure would, however, appear to be open to serious statistical criticism, as it does not allow for correlations between saving rates and the other exogenous variables. As a result, it only allows saving to influence investment to the extent that their covariation is uncorrelated with other exogenous variables.

6 Tesar (1991) gives a particularly comprehensive set of empirical results.

7 Australia, Austria, Belgium, Canada, Denmark, Finland, France, Germany, Greece, Ireland, Italy, Japan, the Netherlands, New Zealand, Norway, Portugal, Spain, Sweden, Switzerland, Turkey, the United Kingdom, and the United States. Luxembourg was not included because its data are known to behave in a very different manner (Tesar, 1991), presumably reflecting its small size and currency union (which includes

unfettered capital movements) with Belgium. Indeed, given this fact, the observation that Luxembourg behaves differently from the remainder of the sample provides some evidence that high capital mobility is indeed associated with lower correlations between saving and investment.

8 Dooley *et al.* (1987) looked at saving–investment correlations for developing countries and found them to be smaller than those for industrial countries, in spite of the general belief that these countries are unable to use private markets very effectively because of borrowing constraints. This lower coefficient may well reflect the fact that many capital flows to developing countries from official sources are not based on market returns, as is assumed in the Feldstein–Horioka test. It would be interesting for developing countries to investigate the correlation between a definition of saving which included foreign official flows and investment. This would be a better way of approaching the underlying issue being tested by Feldstein and Horioka, namely whether or not net private capital flows are large in comparison with underlying saving rates, than using the Feldstein–Horioka regression.

9 The mechanism in this paper is very similar to the time-series model discussed by Obstfeld.

10 Regressions using data across regions of the world economy, in particular Europe and East Asia, also show a fall in the coefficient over time (Bayoumi and Sterne, 1993).

11 This conclusion has not been universally shared (Tesar (1991) discusses these issues). Further evidence is provided below.

12 Obviously, these arguments would not hold if the time-series data are dominated by trends rather than cycles. But this appears unlikely as investment is known to be the most variable component of spending over the cycle.

13 The data come from the Canadian *Provincial Economic Accounts*.

14 It also implies that using panel estimation techniques on saving–investment data is not particularly helpful. If the time-series and cross-sectional correlations reflect different types of behavior, then panel results will fail to provide any improvement in estimation.

15 Clearly, there are some issues to do with boundary conditions which would need to be dealt with. I simply offer this model as an example of how a theoretical mechanism producing a negative correlation between saving and investment could be generated.

16 Alberta, British Columbia, Manitoba, New Brunswick, Newfoundland, Nova Scotia, Ontario, Prince Edward Island, Quebec, and Saskatchewan. The data come from the Canadian *Provincial National Accounts*.

17 The federal fiscal system in Canada is described in Boadway and Hobson (1993). Bayoumi and Masson (1995) provide an analysis of the role of federal taxes and grants across Canadian provinces.

18 As has already been noted, Obstfeld (1986) used evidence from the gold standard period to argue that the time-series correlations observed in the data did not reflect low capital mobility.

19 In the 34 years between 1880 and 1913 the United Kingdom ran an average current account surplus of 4.5 percent of GDP, and Australia an almost equally large deficit (Bayoumi, 1990, Table 6).

20 Eichengreen (1990).

21 The Japanese data do not start until 1885. However, this is not a significant problem as the classical gold standard period is generally argued to start in 1880, the year after the United States returned to the gold standard after suspension in 1862 caused by the US Civil War.

22 The Canadian data exclude federal government saving.

23 Mussa *et al.* (1994). Tesar (1995) provides evidence that although gross transactions have risen over time, net positions have stayed relatively stable.

24 Eichengreen (1995).

25 Bayoumi and Sterne (1993) report such correlations for Europe and East Asia. We find that the correlations across regions tend to be lower than across all countries, presumably reflecting the fact that closer trade ties and cultural connections make regional imbalances easier to accept politically than those with more distant countries. They also show a fall in correlations over time. Indeed, for the most recent period we found no correlation between saving and investment within the European Union.

26 See Obstfeld and Rogoff (1996, Chapter 6) and the last chapter for examples of such models.

4 Consumption and international capital mobility

Much of the recent work on international capital mobility has focused on comparisons of the path of consumption across countries. The connection with capital mobility comes from the desire of individuals to smooth consumption. As streams of income vary over time, people have an incentive to use capital markets to borrow and lend so as to achieve a preferable path for consumption. Successful consumption smoothing, therefore, implies active use of assets markets. The same logic can be applied to comparisons of consumption across countries. The desire to smooth consumption over time is an incentive for countries to use international capital markets to deviate from the path of consumption implied by a country's domestic resources. The degree to which countries succeed in smoothing consumption can therefore be seen as a measure of the degree of access that they have to capital markets.

Tests of capital mobility based on consumption smoothing (called the 'risk sharing' hypothesis, as consumers use asset markets to reduce risk) have a number of similarities with those based on saving–investment correlations, which were discussed in the last chapter. Both are derived from the predictions of macroeconomic models, and involve comparing observed conduct to that derived from such models assuming international capital mobility to be high or low. The validity of the conclusions about capital mobility therefore depends upon the validity of the underlying macroeconomic model. In addition, as these macroeconomic models generally assume a representative consumer, the focus is on *net* capital flows across countries rather than their gross counterparts.

At the same time, there are also significant differences between the two literatures. On the one hand, the underlying theory for the work based on consumption smoothing is stronger than that for saving–investment correlations, so that the literature suffers from fewer theoretical ambiguities. In addition, as consumption is the ultimate goal of economic activity, testing the degree to which financial markets are used to improve its path over time is in some respects a more fundamental test of the beneficial effects of financial integration than those based on correlations of saving and investment across countries (or comparisons of offshore and onshore nominal interest rates). The impact of government policies on the behavior is also less of a concern. Macroeconomic policy is not likely to be directed at producing a target value for private consumption in the way that it may have been used to achieve a target value for the current account, and hence the difference between saving and investment.

On the other hand, there is considerable empirical evidence that individual consumers within countries (who clearly operate in a local environment of high capital mobility) do not fully smooth consumption.[1] It is therefore important when using international consumption patterns to test for the level of international capital mobility to compare observed behavior across countries with equivalent consumption patterns in environments where capital mobility is known to be high, such as within a country.

Before discussing the theoretical and empirical literature on international risk sharing in more detail, mention should be made of a related literature, namely that on the intertemporal approach to the balance of payments.[2] In many ways, this can be seen as the flip-side of the work on international consumption patterns. Instead of focusing on the implications of utility maximization for the path of consumption over time, the intertemporal approach looks at the implications of such behavior for the path of the external balance.[3] As any change in the current account requires an offsetting international capital flow, this work can also be seen as testing for the degree of capital mobility. However, with some notable exceptions,[4] this connection has not been made in the literature. Accordingly, rather than surveying the entire literature, I will confine myself to discussing the pertinent papers in the appropriate places.

Theory

Within a financially integrated area, individuals with access to capital markets can use them to smooth their consumption in response to idiosyncratic movements in income.[5] The most important result from this literature is that in a world of full contingent markets and perfect information, consumption growth across different individuals (or, in our case, countries) should be highly correlated. To see why this is so, first consider the familiar Euler equation, which characterizes the consumption behavior of a rational, forward-looking, individual with access to capital markets, first formulated by Hall (1978):

$$E_{t-1}\{(U'(C_t)/U'(C_{t-1}))(\beta/(1+R_{t-1}))\} = 1 \qquad (4.1)$$

where $U(.)$ is a utility function, C_t is consumption, E_{t-1} is the mathematical expectation conditional on the information available at t-1, β is a subjective discount factor, and R_{t-1} is the real interest rate between t-1 and t. The equation says that individuals will use their access to capital markets to equate the expected marginal utility of consumption over time, adjusted for the real interest rate and a subjective discount rate.

Making the assumptions that the utility function is time separable, has a constant elasticity of intertemporal substitution (so $U=C_t^{1-\mu}$), and that the errors are log-normal, the solution to the model is:

$$\Delta c_t = \mu(\sigma^2_{t+1}/2) + \mu^{-1}\ln(\beta(1+R_{t-1})) + \varepsilon_t \qquad (4.2)$$

where c_t is $\log(C_t)$, σ^2_{t+1} is the variance of future shocks to the logarithm of consumption, R_t is the real interest rate, and the error ε_t, which represents unexpected revisions to permanent income, should be orthogonal to all information known at t-1 or earlier.[6]

If countries are in a financially integrated area, and therefore face the same real interest rate, equation (4.2) implies:

$$\Delta c_{at} = \mu(\sigma_a^2/2) + \mu^{-1}\ln(\beta(1+R_{t-1})) + \varepsilon_{at}$$
$$\Delta c_{bt} = \mu(\sigma_b^2/2) + \mu^{-1}\ln(\beta(1+R_{t-1})) + \varepsilon_{bt} \qquad (4.3)$$
$$\vdots$$
$$\Delta c_{rt} = \mu(\sigma_r^2/2) + \mu^{-1}\ln(\beta(1+R_{t-1})) + \varepsilon_{rt}$$

where subscripts a, b ... r represent consumption across different countries. Equations (4.3) assume that countries have the same utility function, and, in particular, that they have the same intertemporal elasticity of substitution (μ^{-1}) and subjective discount rate (β).

The central insight of the literature on consumption risk sharing is that unexpected changes to permanent income, and hence the errors in equations (4.3), should be the same across countries, except for shocks to tastes or measurement error. This follows from the desire of individuals to insure themselves as fully as possible against unexpected changes in their circumstances, which produces an incentive to use asset markets to reduce the changes in permanent income they face. In the limiting case of full and costless contingent markets and full information, all such idiosyncratic risk will be avoided. As global risk cannot be insured, there will still be unexpected revisions to permanent income, but such changes will be identical across all countries. In terms of the equations above, all of the errors (ε_{at}, ε_{bt}, etc.) will be (almost) perfectly correlated, and hence all the σ_i^2s will also be the same across countries.

This model produces a very simple and testable hypothesis. *Consumption growth across countries will be identical, except for measurement errors and unexpected disturbances to tastes.* An alternative derivation of this result is to consider the path for consumption which would be chosen by a benign social planner.[7] For any given trajectory for aggregate consumption across all individuals, the Pareto optimal solution for each individual or country involves identical comovements in consumption.[8] This is an example of the more general result that the competitive outcome in a world of complete markets and common information is Pareto optimal, and hence identical to the solution with a benign social planner.

Even if markets are not complete, there are still incentives to avoid idiosyncratic risk. Hence, changes in permanent income across countries will still have a significant common element. Idiosyncratic changes in permanent income, however, will reduce the correlation of consumption across countries. Even in this model, however, changes in consumption across countries should still be independent of predictable changes in all variables, except real interest rates. As differential changes in income across countries due to cyclical factors are relatively predictable, this probably still implies a relatively high correlation of consumption across countries.

Empirical evidence

Table 4.1 presents some evidence on the correlation of consumption and real GDP across 21 OECD countries between 1973 and 1990.[9] It reports the correlation between the growth of domestic consumption

Table 4.1 Correlations of consumption and real GDP growth across 21 OECD countries, 1973–90

	Correlation between domestic consumption growth and consumption in other countries	*Correlation between domestic consumption growth and domestic GDP growth*	*Correlation between domestic GDP growth and GDP growth in the rest of the region*
Australia	0.36	0.73	0.55
Austria	0.20	0.68	0.45
Belgium	0.49	0.80	0.51
Canada	0.53	0.95	0.71
Denmark	0.56	0.78	0.52
Finland	0.42	0.25	0.10
France	0.39	0.55	0.58
Germany	0.56	0.65	0.78
Greece	-0.20	0.23	0.42
Ireland	0.57	0.75	0.41
Italy	0.29	0.88	0.56
Japan	0.48	0.69	0.57
The Netherlands	0.37	0.52	0.65
Norway	0.08	0.70	0.21
New Zealand	0.12	0.70	0.23
Portugal	0.12	0.73	0.41
Spain	0.34	0.93	0.34
Sweden	0.43	0.48	0.12
Switzerland	0.26	0.93	0.44
United Kingdom	0.49	0.77	0.71
United States	0.62	0.88	0.68

See the text for an explanation.

and the growth of consumption in the other 20 countries, plus the correlation with domestic real GDP. The results are sharply at odds with the simple theory of consumption risk sharing outlined above, a result also found by other authors using similar calculations.[10] There is a positive correlation between domestic and foreign consumption growth, but the observed correlation is considerably lower than the near-perfect correlation predicted by the full insurance model. In addition, the correlation between the growth in domestic consumption and domestic real GDP is almost universally larger than the correlation between the growth of home and foreign consumption, implying that domestic output is generally a better predictor of home consumption than foreign consumption. Finally, output growth across countries is generally more highly correlated than consumption growth.[11] These observations have been described in the international real business cycle literature (which assumes perfect international capital mobility and full contingent markets) as a major empirical anomaly.[12]

A more formal way of testing the simple risk-sharing hypothesis is through the type of regression first proposed by Mace (1991), who looked at the evidence for full insurance behavior on data for consumption across individuals in the United States. Her insight was that the equilibrium path for consumption for any individual could be proxied by the change in aggregate consumption. Accordingly, no other variables should significantly influence consumption once the change in aggregate consumption is included in the regression. Her regression equation was therefore:

$$\Delta c_{it} = \alpha + \beta\, X_{it} + \Psi\, \Delta c_{A't} + \varepsilon_{it} \qquad (4.4)$$

where Δc_{it} is the change in consumption for individual i, X_{it} is a vector of individual characteristics, such as the change in disposable income or unemployment, and $\Delta c_{A't}$ is the change in consumption across all other members of the panel. Her test of full insurance was that the coefficients on individual characteristics (β) should be zero, while that on aggregate consumption (Ψ) should be unity. She found significant, if relatively small, deviations from full insurance.[13]

The same approach can be used to look at consumption behavior across countries. The main issue is deciding which country-specific terms (the X_{it}s) should be included in equation (4.4). Obstfeld (1995) suggests measuring capital mobility by including the change in domestic resources available for consumption, defined as total output (GDP) less investment and government consumption, in the regression. The logic behind this term is that in a world of financial autarky, in which domestic consumers have no access to international capital markets, the growth in domestic consumption would necessarily equal the growth in available domestic resources. The higher the coefficient on domestic resources in equation (4.4), therefore, the greater will be the degree to which countries fail to use international capital markets to smooth consumption, while the coefficient on the growth of foreign consumption measures the degree to which countries engage in such international risk sharing.[14]

Other authors have suggested other approaches and country-specific variables to test the simple model of international risk sharing. Lewis (1996a), for example, uses time dummies to take out the common element in consumption movements across countries, and focuses on the relationship between the remaining part of consumption and deviations of real GDP from its common element. Ubide (1994) estimates vector autoregressions (VARs) across different members of the European Union (EU) and compares their responses to different types of external and domestic disturbances. Canova and Ravn (1994) use generalized methods of moments estimators to look at some of the implied orthogonality conditions across countries, while Bayoumi and MacDonald (1995) use a similar econometric approach to differentiate potential reasons for low levels of net capital flows across countries.

I focus upon the Obstfeld approach because, as will become apparent later, it appears to be a relatively good test for the existence of capital mobility. This does not mean, however, that this equation is necessarily the best empirical description of international consumption patterns. Other country-specific variables, such as real GDP or disposable income, may well also matter.

Accordingly, the following version of equation (4.4) was estimated:

$$\Delta c_{it} = \alpha_i + \beta \ \Delta(y\text{-}i\text{-}g)_{it} + \Psi \ \Delta c_{A't} + \varepsilon_{it} \qquad (4.5)$$

where $\Delta(y\text{-}g\text{-}i)_{it}$ is the change in domestic resources available for consumption and all variables are measured using logarithms. If the economy is completely closed to international financial markets, and hence consumption is forced to follow the path of available resources, the coefficient on income available for consumption (β) will be unity, while that on the change in foreign consumption (Ψ) will be zero. By contrast, if consumption follows the consumption risk-sharing path then changes in domestic resources should be zero ($\beta = 0$), while changes in home consumption should mirror consumption in other countries in the sample except for a random error ($\Psi = 1$). Finally, situations between these two extremes will produce positive coefficients on both variables.

Table 4.2 reports the results from estimating this specification over 1973–90 for 21 industrial countries. Industrial countries were chosen as they generally have reasonably efficient domestic capital markets

Table 4.2 Consumption regression across 21 OECD countries, 1973–90

	Domestic resources	Foreign consumption	Adjusted R^2	Durbin–Watson statistics
Australia	-0.20 (0.28)	0.47 (0.34)	0.05	1.51
Austria	0.75 (0.19)**	0.55 (0.26)*	0.45	2.28
Belgium	0.87 (0.31)**	0.75 (0.33)*	0.43	2.03
Canada	0.74 (0.32)*	0.22 (0.54)	0.40	1.81
Denmark	0.01 (0.34)	1.15 (0.46)*	0.22	1.30
Finland	0.24 (0.25)	0.77 (0.78)	0.13	1.96
France	0.11 (0.21)	0.33 (0.19)	0.06	2.49
Germany	0.23 (0.21)	0.62 (0.24)**	0.28	1.20
Greece	0.68 (0.19)**	0.34 (0.46)	0.42	2.48
Ireland	0.48 (0.13)**	1.83 (0.52)**	0.59	0.98
Italy	0.73 (0.23)**	0.22 (0.28)	0.37	2.07
Japan	0.32 (0.20)	0.74 (0.28)**	0.25	2.16
The Netherlands	0.57 (0.15)**	0.53 (0.25)*	0.50	1.43
Norway	0.11 (0.19)	0.11 (0.83)	-0.10	1.14
New Zealand	0.25 (0.18)	0.29 (0.56)	0.01	1.79
Portugal	1.09 (0.18)**	-0.05 (0.58)	0.72	1.55
Spain	0.88 (0.32)**	0.14 (0.40)	0.34	0.93
Sweden	-0.07 (0.17)	0.64 (0.34)	0.09	1.40
Switzerland	0.24 (0.18)	0.35 (0.27)	0.06	1.55
United Kingdom	1.14 (0.21)**	0.18 (0.32)	0.71	1.44
United States	1.01 (0.34)**	-0.17 (0.56)	0.53	1.19
All countries	0.45 (0.04)**	0.52 (0.10)**	0.31	–
Countries with open capital markets	0.30 (0.05)**	0.47 (0.12)**	0.21	–

Regression: $\Delta c_{it} = \alpha_i + \beta\Delta(y\text{-}i\text{-}g)_{it} + \Psi\Delta c_{A_i} + \varepsilon_{it}$

See the text for an explanation of the regressions. Standard errors are reported in parenthesis.

*Significant at the 5 percent level.
**Significant at the 1 percent level.

and their potential access to international capital markets has generally been high.[15] The coefficient on domestic resources is significantly different from zero for 11 out of the 21 individual country regressions. For several of these countries, for example Greece, Italy, Portugal, and Spain, the significant coefficients on domestic resources may be explained by the presence of government controls on international capital movements over the estimation period. In other cases, however, capital controls do not appear to be a factor. Both the United States and Canada have large and significant coefficients on domestic resources despite having had virtually no controls on access to international capital markets throughout the period.

The coefficient on foreign consumption is significant for seven countries, rather fewer than the number with significant coefficients on home resources. Four of these countries also have significant coefficients on domestic resources, implying that capital markets are being partially used to smooth consumption. Only in the cases of Denmark, Germany, and Japan are the results consistent with the coefficient constraints implied by full international risk sharing of consumption. Finally, for a significant number of countries, such as Australia, Norway, and Switzerland, neither coefficient is significant – the estimation model simply does not explain consumption very well.

One reason for the lack of significance of many of the coefficients may be the limited number of data points for individual countries. Accordingly, Table 4.2 also reports panel regressions in which the data for individual countries are stacked into a single panel regression. The first such regression, which includes data from all 21 countries, provides a way of summarizing average behavior across the sample. The coefficient on domestic resources in this regression implies that on average 45 percent of the change in consumption is associated with changes in domestic resources, while 52 percent is associated with foreign consumption. On average, therefore, these results show OECD countries as a whole to be about half way between the two extremes of no capital mobility and full consumption risk sharing. The restriction that the coefficients are the same across all countries (not reported), however, is rejected, indicating that significant differences in behavior exist across countries.

The second panel regression excludes eight countries which imposed significant capital controls through the estimation period.[16] Changes in home resources explain 30 percent of the change in consumption in this more limited sample, rather than the 45 percent found for the full sample, while changes in foreign consumption continue to explain about half the variation. The restriction that the coefficients are equal across all countries can be accepted for this regression, indicating that these 'open' countries have relatively homogenous behavior.

The fall in the estimated coefficient on domestic resources is consistent with the idea that this coefficient provides a measure of access to international capital markets, although the fact that the coefficient on this variable continues to be highly significant indicates that the use of these markets to smooth consumption is far from complete, even for countries with relatively open capital markets. The similarity of the coefficients on foreign consumption across the two panel regressions should also be noted. It suggests that while countries without capital controls have used their increased access to international capital markets to alter consumption, this alteration may not have been exclusively toward the full international smoothing of consumption implied by the risk sharing model.

Other authors who have looked at consumption correlations across countries have also concluded that consumption patterns across countries are inconsistent with the simple version of the risk sharing model due-to excess sensitivity to domestic variables, for example Obstfeld (1995), Lewis (1996a), and van Wincoop (1995). Obstfeld and Lewis also concur with the conclusion that capital controls make consumption more sensitive to domestic variables. Lewis reports higher estimated coefficients on the change in real GDP for countries with capital controls than for countries without them. Obstfeld tests for the impact of capital controls by comparing coefficients on domestic resources across different time periods. He finds that the estimated coefficients tend to be higher from 1951–72 compared with 1973–88, which is consistent with the greater pervasiveness of controls during the 1950s and 1960s.[17]

The failure of the simple model of consumption risk sharing, even in the case of countries with open capital markets, and the related observation that portfolios are highly weighted toward domestic assets[18] have produced a number of alternative explanations.[19] Most of these assume high capital mobility, but suggest a mechanism by which income and consumption can still be correlated. For example, Baxter and Crucini (1994) look at the structure of assets markets. In a real business cycle framework, they compare behavior with complete asset markets with behavior when international financial transactions are limited to fixed interest rate debt. The results depend crucially on the nature of the underlying productivity disturbances. If these disturbances are highly persistent but temporary, the change in access to assets has little impact on the model. If these disturbances are permanent (i.e. the process is a random walk), then the correlation between movements in home and foreign consumption is negative, at least in their particular example. It should be noted, however, that a world in which underlying disturbances between countries are permanent is (presumably) one in which the incentive to use contingent assets markets would be large. No explanation is offered as to why debt is freely traded while contingent claims such as equity are difficult to trade in circumstances where they would be useful.

A second type of explanation revolves around non-separabilities in the utility function. The theory discussed earlier assumed that utility depends only upon total consumption. Adding leisure to the utility function, so that there is a trade-off between consumption and hours worked, can generate a positive correlation between output and consumption. Increases in the desired level of work compared with leisure (caused, for example, by a change in the real hourly wage) will be compensated by increases in the level of desired consumption. The existing real business cycle literature which incorporates this mechanism, however, indicates that labor–leisure trade-offs do not fundamentally change consumption risk sharing.[20] A similar type of result can be produced by dividing consumption between traded and nontraded goods. An increase in the availability of nontraded goods will generate a complementary increase in consumption of traded goods, again leading to a correlation between output and consumption. Non-separabilities between durable and nondurable goods can have similar consequences.

Lewis (1996a) takes a comprehensive empirical look at the potential explanatory power of non-separabilities in a paper which considers behavior across a wide range of developed and developing countries. Changes in unemployment (used as a proxy for hours worked) and differentiating between durable and nondurable goods do not significantly affect the estimated dependence of the growth of consumption on the growth in real output. Distinguishing between traded and nontraded goods (in addition to taking account of the impact of capital controls), however, makes the residual dependence of the growth of consumption in traded goods upon the growth of real output of traded goods insignificant.[21]

Hence, Lewis found that non-separabilities between traded and nontraded goods can fully explain the correlation between consumption and income, even if capital mobility is high. It would be interesting to see what kind of correlations between the growth in consumption and output of traded goods occur in models in which price rigidities, market imperfections, and rules of thumb are important, in other words, to see if the test has a high level of power with regard to reasonable alternatives. In the absence of such information, the results indicate that separabilities in utility functions explain how consumption and income *could* be correlated in general equilibrium with complete markets, but do not necessarily indicate that the risk sharing model is correct.

The final explanation of the high correlation between consumption and income revolves around the idea that the gains from international risk sharing are too small to outweigh the costs of creating an international portfolio. Cole and Obstfeld (1991), Obstfeld (1992), and Tesar (1995) all suggest that the gain to lifetime utility from consumption smoothing may be relatively small, and hence that consumers may not find it worth using asset markets to provide insurance. This view has been disputed, however, most notably by van Wincoop (1995), who finds significantly higher costs from failing to diversify across countries. The view that the gains from asset market trade are small is also inconsistent with an earlier finance literature pointing to significant gains from portfolio diversification across countries. Lewis (1996b) provides a discussion of the differing assumptions used in these two literatures, without coming to any firm conclusion as to which set of assumptions is correct.[22] Clearly, this issue is still open to considerable debate.

The overall approach of comparing the costs and benefits of risk sharing can be used to look at more general market inefficiencies than simply the costs of transactions. The simplest way of introducing capital controls into a model is to see them as an additional cost which consumers have to bear in order to make an international transaction.[23] This formalizes the argument as to why capital controls produce excess sensitivity to changes in domestic resources. Uncertainty as to the future behavior of governments with respect to capital flows, which has been discussed in the last two chapters as a possible reason for limited net capital flows across countries, could have the same effect, as could other potential inefficiencies, such as differing legal codes, exchange rate uncertainty, or lower levels of information. If these costs outweigh the benefits from risk sharing then the solution will look like that produced by capital controls, with limited net capital flows between nations. The resolution of these alternative explanations of the failure of the simple risk sharing model lies in the future. A useful first step, however, is to compare international consumption patterns with the same behavior when capital mobility is known to be high. Consumption across Canadian provinces provides an obvious way of doing this. Canada has a unified capital market and no significant restrictions on intra-national transactions in assets. In addition, it is a sufficiently large country geographically for the distinction between traded and nontraded goods across provinces likely to be similar to that between countries.[24] In these important dimensions, therefore, Canada would appear to be a good comparator for international behavior.

At the same time, account needs to be taken of some of the differences in the situation of provinces within the Canadian federation as opposed to countries within the industrial world. The most important is probably the existence of a federal tax system which reallocates resources across provinces. Such transfers need to be taken into account when calculating the path of domestic resources available for consumption. Fortunately, in addition to reporting data on consumption across provinces, the Canadian *Provincial Economic Accounts* also report estimates of federal net lending by province. Accordingly, in the results that follow, the path of provincial domestic resources is adjusted by the difference between net lending of the federal government within the province and average net lending across all provinces. This allows for the transfer element of federal fiscal policy.

Another difference between provinces and countries is that financial transactions within Canada do not require any change in currency, with its associated transaction costs. This difference could mean that consumers would be prepared to use domestic markets to smooth consumption across provinces, but would be unwilling to use external markets in the same way because of the extra costs involved. In practice, however, charges for wholesale foreign exchange transactions appear small relative, for example, to the costs of acquiring assets such as stocks or bonds. In addition, transaction costs for securities are likely to be lower in high-volume markets, such as New York, than for the smaller Canadian equivalents. Any change in conduct caused by exchange rate transaction costs is thus likely to be small.

Table 4.3 Correlations of consumption and GPP growth across the 10
Canadian provinces, 1972–93

	Correlation between growth of domestic consumption and consumption in the rest of the country	Correlation between growth of domestic consumption and domestic GPP		Correlation between growth of domestic GPP and GPP in the rest of the country	
British Columbia	0.75	0.92	(0.94)	0.88	(0.82)
Alberta	0.59	0.80	(0.73)	0.64	(0.43)
Saskatchewan	0.80	0.76	(0.68)	0.69	(0.63)
Manitoba	0.83	0.88	(0.83)	0.92	(0.89)
Ontario	0.88	0.91	(0.94)	0.81	(0.76)
Quebec	0.92	0.85	(0.90)	0.92	(0.86)
New Brunswick	0.81	0.70	(0.47)	0.84	(0.50)
Prince Edward Island	0.71	0.61	(0.45)	0.70	(0.58)
Nova Scotia	0.91	0.85	(0.58)	0.75	(0.39)
Newfoundland	0.82	0.68	(0.46)	0.57	(0.59)

The numbers in parenthesis refer to GPP not adjusted by net federal lending to the
province.

Table 4.3 reports correlations of the growth in consumption with
real GPP (the provincial equivalent of GDP) across different Canadian
provinces. All the correlations across Canadian provinces appear
higher than the equivalent values across countries (Table 4.1). The
importance of taking net transfers of resources across provinces into
account is also underlined by the generally higher correlations between domestic consumption and real GPP after such transfers are
taken into account (results with the unadjusted data are reported in
parentheses). In many cases the correlation of provincial consumption
with consumption in the rest of the country is higher than the
correlation with domestic output, whereas in the international data the
opposite was almost universally true. This suggests that the behavior
of consumption may well be quantitatively different between the two
data sets.

The results from estimating equation (4.5) across the 10 provinces
in Canada individually, as well as a panel regression across all
provinces, are reported in Table 4.4. The coefficient restrictions implied by high capital in the risk sharing model are almost universally

68 *Capital mobility*

Table 4.4 Consumption correlations across the 10 Canadian provinces, 1972–93

	Domestic resources		Consumption in the rest of Canada		Adjusted R^2	Durbin–Watson statistics
Alberta	0.09	(0.08)	0.99	(0.32)**	0.33	2.01
British Columbia	-0.09	(0.11)	1.07	(0.25)**	0.53	1.17
Manitoba	0.01	(0.06)	0.85	(0.13)**	0.66	1.79
New Brunswick	-0.01	(0.04)	0.79	(0.14)**	0.62	1.70
Newfoundland	0.10	(0.05)	0.74	(0.17)**	0.70	1.87
Nova Scotia	0.02	(0.05)	1.01	(0.12)**	0.82	1.74
Ontario	-0.07	(0.08)	0.96	(0.14)**	0.76	0.58
Prince Edward Island	-0.10	(0.07)	1.12	(0.23)**	0.50	2.02
Quebec	-0.18	(0.05)**	1.20	(0.08)**	0.91	1.81
Saskatchewan	0.05	(0.04)	0.92	(0.15)**	0.64	1.58
Panel of all provinces	0.02	(0.02)	0.92	(0.06)**	0.58	n.a.

$\Delta c_{it} = \alpha + \beta\ \Delta(y\text{-}i\text{-}g)_{it} + \Psi\ \Delta c_{CA't} + \varepsilon_{it}$
See the text for an explanation of the regressions. Standard errors are reported in parentheses.
**Significant at the 1 percent level.

accepted. The coefficients on domestic resources are small and insignificantly different from zero, while those on consumption in the rest of the nation are large, highly significantly different from zero, and insignificantly different from unity. (The one exception is Quebec, where the coefficient on domestic resources is significantly negative, and that on consumption in the rest of the country is larger than unity, the opposite of what would be expected with low capital mobility.)

The results indicate that the suggested coefficient restrictions on equation (4.5) discussed by Obstfeld appear to be a good test of capital mobility. In a situation of high capital mobility, consumption does indeed appear to be independent of the path of domestic resources, as postulated by Obstfeld.[25] The provincial Canadian results are particularly interesting, as Canada is a country where the coefficient on domestic resources is large and significant in the international results reported in Table 4.2. Canadians appear to smooth consumption successfully with regard to changes in resources across provinces, but much less so with respect to similar disturbances between Canada and the rest of the world.[26]

The results help to shed light on the alternative explanations for the dependence of consumption on domestic resources outlined earlier. The clear difference in the behavior of consumption across countries and across Canadian provinces implies that international consumption patterns in all probability do not simply reflect equilibrium responses in a world of perfect markets and separabilities in the utility function, as suggested by Lewis (1996a). They are also difficult to reconcile with differences in access to conventional debt and other types of financial claims, unless these differences reflect other market imperfections which differ across countries but not within a country. Rather, they suggest a world in which the costs of international capital movements are too high to make risk sharing across countries worthwhile. Transactions costs could explain this lack of diversification. However, the fact that individuals within Canada apparently find domestic risk sharing worthwhile makes it less likely that transactions costs alone explain behavior across countries. Other costs, reflecting uncertainties about future government actions, exchange rate risk, or limited information would appear most likely also to be involved.

If the basic premise is accepted, that net capital flows across countries are 'too small' compared with a world of high capital mobility and low transactions costs, a further issue which can be explored is the reason for this failure. Two alternative reasons are possible: national capital markets could be sufficiently separated that real interest rates differ significantly across countries; alternatively, international capital markets could be integrated, but various costs to international financial intermediation could make consumption excessively correlated with local income. Bayoumi and MacDonald (1995) propose a way of differentiating these alternative hypotheses. After allowing for the excess correlation of changes in consumption with (predictable) changes in disposable income, we consider the relationship between the remaining part of consumption at home and abroad. We find that changes in income provide the main explanation for deviations of consumption from its desired path. However, there is also evidence that real interest rates in several European countries, many of which had significant capital controls over the estimation period, were not fully integrated with the rest of the world.[27]

Conclusion

The literature on international consumption patterns is still in a formative stage, and any general conclusions drawn are, inevitably, speculative. New theoretical insights which transform the way that we look at the existing evidence appear much more likely to occur in the realm of tests of capital mobility based on consumption than on tests using comparisons of nominal interest rates or of correlations between saving and investment across countries. Having said that, the existing results, including those presented in this chapter, point to a fairly limited use of international capital markets to smooth consumption across countries. True, consumption paths since 1973 deviate from the path implied by complete financial autarky in a manner which is much more difficult to discern over the 20 years before 1973. However, the international results do not appear to resemble closely those observed across Canadian provinces. The importance of the path of domestic resources in the international consumption regressions, in contrast to their lack of importance in the Canadian provincial regressions, points to continuing restrictions on risk sharing between countries, and hence low capital mobility.

Support for this conclusion is also provided by the similarities between the results for consumption and for saving–investment correlations, discussed in the last chapter. Indeed, the two literatures have many parallels. In both cases, the initial results indicated unusually small levels of net capital flows across countries compared with what might be expected from a simple model of the economy with high capital mobility. Considerable theoretical ingenuity was then expended on showing how these results could be consistent with high levels of international capital market integration. Such theoretical speculation is indispensable in any academic discipline. However, empirical tests of theories are also indispensable. One of the objectives of this chapter, and of the last, has been to use natural experiments to differentiate between alternative theoretical models.

The results, at least in my reading, indicate that the original intuition was correct, namely that capital flows between countries are indeed significantly lower than might be expected if international capital markets were as highly integrated as those across regions within a country. This conclusion is also supported by other work which indicates that other types of economic integration between countries is considerably more limited than that within countries. For example, tests using the gravity specification indicate that levels of trade between countries are much smaller than would be expected from trade within them.[28] Similarly, evidence on prices indicates that, measured in a common currency, prices of different goods within countries are more closely connected than prices of the same goods between countries.[29] The overall conclusion would appear to be that national and currency boundaries are an important impediment to the free flow of both capital and goods between individuals. The global economy appears to have some troubles at border crossings.

Notes

1 A survey of the microeconomic evidence on consumption behavior for individuals within the United States is provided in Browning and Lusardi (1996). Bayoumi (1995) finds changes in current income to matter significantly for consumption across Canadian provinces, but concludes that the risk sharing hypothesis is still a relatively good description of the data.

2 See Obstfeld and Rogoff (1994) for a survey.

3 See Sachs (1981) for a particularly clear derivation of the basic approach.

4 Ghosh and Ostry (1992), Ghosh (1995), and Bayoumi and Klein (1995).

5 Individuals are also able to smooth income in a world of full contingent markets. Atkeson and Bayoumi (1993) provide empirical estimates of the degree to which individuals actually use assets markets to smooth fluctuations in local income in the United States and EU. See also Asdrubali *et al.* (1996).

6 The term in the variance of future consumption has been of some importance in recent microeconomic work. See the survey on recent microeconomic work on consumption in Browning and Lusardi (1996). Ghosh and Ostry (1992) estimate a model in which this variance is assumed to vary across countries.

7 This is the approach taken by Obstfeld (1995) and Lewis (1996a).

8 This assumes that the utility functions are identical across individuals and are homothetic.

9 The data come from the Penn World Tables (Summers and Heston, 1991), which calculate totals in real US dollars in PPP exchange rates. All aggregates are calculated using the PPP exchange rates implicit in the Penn data.

10 Backus *et al.* (1992), Obstfeld (1995), Tesar (1995), and van Wincoop (1995).

11 As consumption variability tends to be lower than output variability, this result does not necessarily indicate that no consumption smoothing

occurs. It is, however, striking that the international cycle of output appears to be somewhat more coherent than the equivalent cycle for consumption.

12 Backus *et al.* (1992).

13 The issue of whether the full insurance model can be rejected using panel data on individuals is not settled, with some authors finding significant effects from individual-specific factors and others not. See Browning and Lusardi (1996) for a survey of this literature.

14 A similar basic approach is used by Ghosh (1995) in the context of the intertemporal approach to the current account.

15 Access of many developing countries to international capital was severely restricted during the debt crisis of the 1980s.

16 Capital controls were measured using six indicators reported in *Exchange Arrangements and Exchange Restrictions*, an annual publication of the International Monetary Fund (see Grilli and Milesi-Ferretti (1995) for more details). The excluded countries had an annual average of more than one and a half restrictions over the estimation period. They were Belgium, Denmark, France, Greece, Ireland, Italy, Portugal, and Spain.

17 A similar result can be obtained from the specification used in Table 4.2. When the panel regression is repeated over the 1951–72 period, the coefficient on domestic resources rises to 0.73 while that on foreign consumption falls to 0.13 and becomes insignificant.

18 French and Poterba (1991), and Tesar (1995).

19 This lack of diversification of assets implies that income movements across countries are different. Precautionary saving motives may therefore also help to explain the correlation between consumption and income. The only work I am aware of on this topic is by Ghosh and Ostry (1992), who use the framework of the intertemporal approach to the balance of payments.

20 Backus *et al.* (1992).

21 An increase in output and hence consumption of nontraded goods lowers the marginal utility that they provide. The optimal response to this is to raise consumption of traded goods, so as to bring the ratio between the marginal utilities of traded and nontraded goods back to their original level. Hence, the specific location of these nontraded goods generates differential movements in marginal utilities across countries, thereby allowing consumption and output to be correlated.

22 The underlying difficulty is the inability to get a single set of assumptions about the utility function which reproduces both the behavior of consumption and the behavior of stock returns.

23 Lewis (1996a).

24 To use a classic example, the distances are too large, for example, for most residents of Ontario to want to travel to the neighboring provinces for a haircut.

25 This does not necessarily mean that the full insurance model is confirmed. Consumption may well depend on other province-specific variables which are not included in the regression.

26 Focusing specifically on Canada, Bayoumi and Klein (1995) come to a very similar conclusion using the intertemporal approach to the balance of payments. Trade balances across Canadian provinces appear to follow the intertemporal model very closely, while the trade balance between Canada and the rest of the world responds only partially to these intertemporal factors.

27 For our sample, these were Austria, Belgium and Luxembourg, Denmark, Greece, Italy, and the Netherlands.

28 McCallum (1995) tests the model using data on trade for individual Canadian provinces. Wei (1996) uses a similar specification but looks at overall trade within and between different countries.

29 See, for example, Froot *et al.* (1995), who use data going back to 1273, and Engel and Rogers (1994), who estimate the 'width' of the Canadian border using price data.

Optimum currency areas

5 The theory of optimum currency areas

Money is one of humanity's greatest innovations. Its most important characteristic, as every economics textbook notes, is that it solves the problem of the double coincidence of wants. I do not have to go and find people who both want a book on economics and can offer me things which I want (food, clothing, shelter). Nor do people who wish to buy this book have to worry about my needs. Money separates these transactions and, as a store of value which can be traded for goods, is the lubricant which greases modern economies. However, we do not all use the same money. A New Yorker uses US dollars, as do Los Angelenos. But Londoners use pounds sterling, inhabitants of Tokyo yen, and Berliners deutsche marks.

The theory of optimum currency areas looks at the advantages and disadvantages of different regions adopting the same currency.[1] A single currency simplifies transactions across regions by guaranteeing a fixed rate of exchange. A New Yorker visiting California can buy things without having to worry about the rate of exchange between 'New York' dollars and 'Californian' dollars. The same is clearly not true of a New Yorker visiting London, as the dollar value of goods depends upon both the local price in pounds and on the rate of exchange between the dollar and the pound. The additional step of changing dollars for pounds involves both uncertainty, as the rate of exchange between the two currencies can change, and cost, as third parties have to be used in the transaction. However, the convenience of a single currency has to be weighed against its cost. The great advantage of having separate monies is that local interest and exchange rates can vary with local conditions. The same is not true within a currency union. Because they have the same currency and hence a fixed exchange rate, regions also have the same (riskless) interest rate.[2]

It is worth noting at the outset that the analysis of optimum currency areas is relatively recent, reflecting, at least in part, changes in the nature of money. When money was generally made up of things of intrinsic worth, most notably precious metals such as gold and silver, the rate of exchange between such coins was determined by the amounts of specie they contained. The choice of which money to use was generally one of little importance, and many types of money circulated in the same place at any one time.[3] As the need for money grew, however, gold and silver started being replaced by paper (or coins made of cheap metals).[4] This is the situation we have today, in which monies are no longer defined in terms of underlying commodities; rather, their value derives from their use in domestic transactions – they are 'legal tender.'[5] The pound sterling is useful in London, but not in New York City, while the US dollar has the opposite characteristic. Since the pound coin and dollar bill have almost no intrinsic value, their rate of exchange can (and does) vary. Thus, as money moved from being composed of valuable specie to valueless paper, the choice of the domestic currency became important as the only way of ensuring stability of the relative value of money between regions.

While many earlier writers had discussed the nature and role of money, the first detailed discussion of optimum currency areas was by Robert Mundell in 'A Theory of Optimum Currency Areas,' a paper in the *American Economic Review* in 1961. It was inspired, at least in part, by the debate then going on about exchange rate policies, with Friedman (1953) arguing that exchange rates should be allowed to float against other currencies. Mundell was trying, among other things, to look at the circumstances in which a fixed exchange rate would be the correct economic policy. He noted that adopting a uniform currency had both advantages and costs, with the advantages stemming from the lower costs of changing money, and its greater value as a medium of exchange.

The core of the paper was taken up by a discussion of the costs of losing monetary flexibility. He noted two factors which could be important in determining the costs of a currency union. The first was the similarity of the underlying economic disturbances. If two regions face similar disturbances, then their desired monetary response will also be similar, and the costs of being forced to set the same nominal interest rate will be small. By contrast, if the regions face dissimilar disturbances – Mundell used the case of the eastern and western halves of the United States and Canada – then a single monetary policy will involve larger costs. Next, he noted that these costs could be solved by another mechanism, namely factor mobility across regions. If labor flowed from the region faced with a negative distur-bance to one faced with a more favorable disturbance, then the economic impact of these diverse disturbances could be solved despite the existence of a single currency. Hence, Mundell stressed high labor mobility as a criterion for deciding the costs of a single currency, and hence the advisability of its adoption.

Mundell's paper has been enormously influential in the literature on optimum currency areas. In addition to posing the original ques-tion, the factors that he identified, the correlation of the underlying shocks and labor mobility, remain central to any discussion of the effects of a currency union. Most subsequent authors have also followed his methodology in several other respects. There remains a focus on factors which influence the costs of losing monetary au-tonomy rather than those which determine the benefits of a single currency, although any assessment of the net impact of forming a currency union involves considering both the costs and benefits of the loss of monetary autonomy. In addition, most of the discussion of optimum currency areas has been relatively informal, an approach also adopted in this survey.[6] A final feature of the literature which derives from Mundell is a tendency for contributors to focus on a single criterion for defining whether a region is an optimum currency area or not. As a result, the literature often has a somewhat disjointed feel.[7] One of the objectives of this survey is to provide an overarching framework in which to consider existing contributions.

At the center of optimum currency area theory is Mundell's original insight on the nature of *the underlying economic disturbances*. If these are small and similar across regions then the costs of adopting a common currency are likely to be relatively minor, regardless of other factors, while if underlying disturbances are large and highly idiosyn-cratic the costs of a common currency are likely to be significant. In addition to the nature of the underlying disturbances, three other broad considerations affect the costs of adopting a single currency. The first is the *efficiency of alternative mechanisms* to the exchange rate for alleviating the impact of idiosyncratic disturbances. These mechanisms include wage and price flexibility, regional mobility of labor and capital, fiscal arrangements, and private capital markets. Second, *the effectiveness of the exchange rate* as a method of alleviating idiosyn-cratic disturbances itself depends upon a number of factors. These include the openness of the economy, industrial diversification of the regions involved, and whether or not the underlying disturbances are regional or industrial. Third, *the desired path for monetary policy* could also vary regionally. Policy makers in different regions could have divergent views about the effectiveness and role of monetary policy, either because of regional differences in economic structure or because of different implicit models. Issues of credibility, and the advantages of tying one's hands, are also relevant in this context.

The discussion will then move on to the smaller literature on the *benefits from a currency union*, before concluding with a short assessment of the current state of the literature and possible avenues for future research.

Underlying disturbances

The central importance of the nature of the underlying economic disturbances in determining the costs of joining a currency union is relatively clear. It is difficult to imagine circumstances in which regions that face small and similar disturbances would be seriously hurt by a currency union.[8] Equally, it would appear highly unlikely that regions subject to large and wildly differing disturbances would wish to form a currency union, or that, if formed, such a union would prove a great success.[9]

The importance of this criterion can be illustrated by looking at examples around the globe. Africa has more countries and currencies than any other continent, and it is the part of the world most dependent on production of commodities for its economic well-being. Commodity markets are subject to large, diverse, and unpredictable disturbances, implying an underlying environment which is probably not conducive to large currency unions.[10] An exception to this rule is the 'CFA' franc zone, made up of 13 French-speaking African states. The economics of the CFA franc zone will be discussed further below.

In the same context, it should come as no surprise that the most enthusiasm for EMU comes from countries such as the Netherlands and Belgium, whose economies are most integrated with that of Germany and very similar to its in structure. Similarly, the lack of enthusiasm for this project in the United Kingdom presumably reflects, at least in part, the lower level of integration of its economy with such core EU members as Germany and the Benelux countries.

The type of disturbances which occur within an area may also be important for its suitability for a currency union. As discussed by Poole (1970), the Mundell–Flemming model of open economies predicts that the impact of real and monetary disturbances on the country or region will vary with the exchange rate regime. Fixed exchange rates, of which monetary union is an extreme version, increase the impact of real disturbances, as there is less crowding out through higher interest rates. By contrast, monetary shocks have less impact in these circumstances. The implication is that the impact of a common currency depends upon the nature of underlying disturbances.[11] Kempa (1995) also differentiates between real and monetary disturbances using a model from a rather different intellectual tradition.[12] Most of the work on optimum currency areas, however, takes underlying real disturbances as given, and focuses on the existence of various mechanisms to reduce the impact of such disturbances.

Nonmonetary mechanisms

While underlying disturbances are an important part of assessing the costs of a currency union, they are not the only factor which should be considered. In particular, there are a number of nonmonetary mechanisms which can reduce the economic disruption caused by idiosyncratic disturbances, and hence reduce the costs of not being able to use the exchange rate to buffer them. The most obvious of these mechanisms is wage and price flexibility. In a world with fully adjustable wages and prices and full information, monetary policy is largely irrelevant for real activity, as domestic and foreign prices adjust immediately. The exchange rate becomes an essentially redundant relative price, as any change in the exchange rate can be replaced by equal changes in all domestic prices.[13] Even with fully flexible prices, monetary policy can still have effects, however, if information is limited. Monetary policy can then operate either through cash-in-advance constraints or through misinterpretation of price signals, as in the Lucas supply function. Alesina and Grilli (1992, 1993) analyze optimum currency area issues in a flexible price model by assuming that the central bank has superior information, which allows it to help stabilize output.[14]

The most natural context in which to think about the issue of optimum currency areas, however, remains a world with nominal price rigidities, as such rigidities provide a clear reason for wishing to have a flexible exchange rate in order to reduce the impact of such rigidities upon the economy. In this case it is clear that the larger the degree of domestic price flexibility, the less is the need for flexibility in the exchange rate. Greater price flexibility therefore makes adopting a single currency easier.

Another mechanism which can help offset idiosyncratic disturbances is labor and capital mobility.[15] An unfavorable regional disturbance lowers the demand for labor and capital in that region (conversely, a favorable disturbance raises demand for these factors of production). One way to regain equilibrium is for labor and capital to move from depressed regions to expanding ones. For example, the economic disruption in an oil-producing region (such as Texas in the United States, or Norway and the north of Scotland in Europe) generated by a fall in world oil prices can be cushioned if labor and capital respond by moving out of the area. Greater labor mobility and, to a lesser extent, capital mobility thus make the formation of a currency union easier.

A third method of cushioning the impact of idiosyncratic regional disturbances is through fiscal policy. Fiscal policy can offset an unfavorable disturbance which lowers the income in a region. Similarly, such 'automatic stabilizers' will tend to reduce income in a region faced with a favorable disturbance. Government fiscal policy can therefore reduce the impact of asymmetric disturbances, and thereby make a currency union easier to maintain. Kenen (1969) was the first to focus on the role of fiscal policy in a currency union, while Sala-i-Martin and Sachs (1992) provide a more recent discussion of the role of automatic stabilizers. One complication with operating automatic stabilizers, not discussed by Sala-i-Martin and Sachs, is that changes in fiscal policy in one region may affect output in neighboring areas. Such fiscal spillover provides an incentive to coordinate fiscal policy across regions, as discussed by Masson and Taylor (1993).

There has also been some recent work on the level of government at which counter-cyclical policies should operate. Bayoumi and Masson (1996) argue that automatic stabilizers are most effective if they are operated at higher levels of government, which, in the case of a currency union, presumably means union-wide. The reason is the reduction in the effectiveness of fiscal stabilization caused by Ricardian effects.[16] A fiscal deficit implies a rise in government debt, and hence a rise in future taxes. Forward-looking individuals will respond to higher debt by increasing their saving, so as to pay for the future taxes, thereby lowering the impact of the deficit in income and activity. Indeed, under some assumptions this rise in private saving will completely offset the government's dissaving.

This Ricardian effect occurs at any level of government. In a federal tax system, however, it is possible that regional shocks within the federation will tend to offset each other. As a result, while a region facing an unfavorable shock may be receiving funds from the federal government, another region with more favorable circumstances may be paying funds into the federal government's coffers. If there is no net impact on the federal budget deficit from all these different regional transfers, then there is no expectation that taxes will rise in the future, and hence no Ricardian offset. Even if there is some change in debt, and hence some Ricardian offset, it is likely to be much smaller than that which would be generated by a similar policy at the local level.

Federal fiscal policies which redistribute income across regions in response to shocks are thus more efficient than the same policies run at a local level. As such insurance is generally simply a function of the structure of the federal fiscal system, it is largely independent of the policies of the government. Clearly, a considerable level of political and social cohesion may be needed to make such a redistribution system politically feasible.[17] This points to the importance of political and social integration in defining the size of an optimum currency area.

A final mechanism which can reduce the impact of idiosyncratic regional disturbances is private capital markets. The intuition can best be illustrated by reference to the Lucas 'coconuts' model.[18] Imagine a world in which everybody starts by owning a coconut tree in their back garden. The number of coconuts produced by each tree has the same statistical distribution, but the amount produced by any one tree in any given year is unpredictable. Assuming that private capital markets are open, the market solution is for each person to own an equal stake in each tree. Hence, if there are 10 people, each owns a one-tenth share in the output of each tree. As a result, although production by each tree is unpredictable, incomes of tree owners are identical. Private capital markets have allowed individuals to hedge all idiosyncratic coconut production risk.

Although private asset markets could, in theory, insure against such risks, there are several features of actual economies which tend to limit the role of private capital markets in providing income insurance. The most basic one is moral hazard. If individuals have fully insured incomes then they have no incentive to work hard. In addition, as wages and salaries are the major source of income for most households and it is not possible to buy and sell labor forward to third parties on organized markets (slavery is illegal), insurance can be achieved only by buying and selling claims on income to capital. The instruments that individuals can purchase may not therefore correspond very closely to the income risk they are likely to experience. Also, much of the wage adjustment that occurs within regions comes through unemployment, and is therefore specific to particular individuals. Finally, stock market gyrations which have little correspondence to current conditions may further reduce the correlation between wage income and returns on assets. These uncertainties mean that any private portfolios directed at insuring against regional disturbances may themselves generate new income uncertainty.

These three types of adjustment mechanisms – price flexibility, resource mobility, and income insurance – operate in somewhat different ways. Consider a region which has been hit by an unfavorable disturbance, so that the demand for labor and capital is less than existing supply, causing unemployment and under-utilization of capacity. Price flexibility works in exactly the same way as the exchange rate. By lowering wages and returns on capital, it helps to revive employment and capital utilization. By contrast, labor and capital mobility solve the problem by allowing resources to flow out of the region. Full employment can thereby be attained with a smaller reduction in wages and prices. Indeed, in the extreme case of full labor and capital mobility, wages and the rate of profit remain equal to their counterparts in other regions as movements in labor and capital equate worldwide factor prices. More generally, these two forms of adjustment work in tandem, with unemployment and low capital utilization encouraging reductions in wages and prices at the same time that they increase the incentive to migrate. The impact of income insurance on this process depends upon its type. Private capital flows and progressive federal personal income taxes may make it easier to accept lower wages, as they provide a partial offset to this reduction in income, while government programs such as unemployment benefit and social safety nets may tend to reduce the incentive to lower wages as they lower the costs of unemployment.

Effectiveness of the exchange rate

A second set of issues which has been discussed in the optimum currency area literature is factors which influence the effectiveness of an independent monetary policy, and hence the exchange rate, as a method of reducing the impact of idiosyncratic disturbances. While monetary policy is undoubtedly a convenient channel through which to deal with differences in the economic fortunes of regions, it is also a relatively blunt instrument. Changes in interest rates and exchange rates affect all those in a region equally, without regard to specific circumstances. The effectiveness of monetary policy as an instrument depends upon the circumstances of the region.

This was recognized in 1963 by Ronald McKinnon, who suggested that openness of the economy to external trade was an important characteristic in determining the value of a currency union.[19] The more open the economy, the greater is the weight of tradeable goods in domestic costs and consumption. As monetary policy has no impact on foreign prices, more open economies experience a larger impact on domestic costs from the exchange rate (through imported raw materials), and hence on prices of domestic goods. In addition, there is a direct effect on living standards through the price of foreign consumption goods. To the extent that individuals resist the erosion of their buying power caused by an exchange rate devaluation by raising domestic wages, this will further erode the impact of the exchange rate on the relative price of domestic and foreign goods. Hence, as an economy becomes more open, the exchange rate becomes less effective at altering relative prices between traded and nontraded goods, and more likely to generate domestic price instability, eroding the usefulness of money as a store of value.

Consider the extreme case, in which I as (say) a widget seller decided to issue my own currency and to transact only in Ballars (short for Bayoumi dollars), and wished to lower my domestic prices by halving the value of the Ballar. The cost of widgets in Ballars would double, as would the prices that I pay for other goods. Overall, the impact of my exchange rate devaluation on the relative price of my widgets would be small. By contrast, the impact of a devaluation of the US dollar has a very different effect, as most of my costs would be in US dollars, and would thus be largely unchanged. The importance of openness to trade on the effectiveness of monetary policy helps to explain why currency unions are generally of a reasonable size, and why very small countries such as the Vatican, Monaco or Liechtenstein, or even Luxembourg and Panama, adopt the currencies of a larger neighboring country.

A very different relationship between openness and optimum currency areas has been suggested more recently by the Commission of the European Communities (1990). The Commission argued that as economies become more integrated through trade, the impact of changes in the exchange rate on the domestic economy becomes larger. Hence, increasing integration produces an incentive to lower exchange rate variability between nations because the output costs of such variability increases.

The types of considerations discussed by the European Commission are probably most relevant for medium to large economies in which imports play an important, but not overwhelming, role. A case in point would be the devaluations of the pound sterling and lira in the wake of the 1992 crisis of the ERM of the European Monetary System, which led to a discussion of the harm that 'competitive' devaluations could have on other members of the EU. Clearly, many other countries regarded these devaluations as providing significant benefits to the countries concerned relative to their close trading partners. In addition to reversing the logic implicit in the McKinnon argument, that openness reduces the impact of monetary policy on the economy, this argument leads to a very different view of the role of the exchange rate. In the Commission's argument the exchange rate is seen less as a method of adjusting to shocks and more as a potential source of such shocks.

Another factor which can affect the usefulness of the exchange rate is industrial structure. Peter Kenen first discussed this issue in a paper written in 1969. He pointed out that it would generally be easier to form a currency union between regions whose industrial structures were relatively diversified, as highly diversified regions are subject to large numbers of disturbances across industries. Assuming that disturbances across specific industries are not highly correlated, the net impact on the region as a whole will tend to be small. Accordingly, the exchange rate is likely to be a less effective tool when applied to a region with a highly diversified industrial base than one with a much narrower set of industries, as the size of the underlying disturbances to the region as a whole is likely to be smaller. Industrial diversification and the nature of underlying disturbances – whether region specific or industry specific – have also been a focus of recent theoretical interest, most notably by Melitz (1991, 1993).

Such an approach raises a number of important issues. The first is that the size of, as well as the correlation between, underlying regional disturbances is important in analyzing the suitability of forming a currency union. The correlation of disturbances across two well diversified regions may well be no larger than across regions which are less diversified. However, as the size of the underlying disturbances are smaller, the regions are better designed to join a currency union. Industrial diversification also highlights the role of intra-industry flexibility within regions in determining the effectiveness of the exchange rate in responding to regional disturbances. If movements of factors of production across industries is difficult, different industries within the same region may well face very divergent economic conditions. Such diversity of experience will reduce the usefulness of the exchange rate in restoring regional equilibrium, as changes in the exchange rate moves all prices within the region by the same amount. Hence, labor mobility between industries within a region may be just as important as mobility between regions in defining a beneficial currency union.

Note, however, that this discussion of the importance of industrial diversity assumes that the disturbances affecting industries in a region are primarily industry-specific. If, by contrast, the disturbances which affect industries are primarily region-specific, reflecting regional business conditions, the importance of industrial structure in determining the nature of the regional disturbances will be diminished, and hence so will the role of industrial diversification in defining an optimum currency area.

Policy implementation

A third broad area of discussion of optimum currency areas has involved the implementation of monetary policy.[20] If policy makers across regions pursue different monetary strategies in response to the same types of disturbance, then there could be costs to forming a currency union, even if the underlying shocks across the regions were very similar. Such differences in policy implementation could reflect either structural differences across regions or differences in the preferences of policy makers about the role and impact of monetary policy.

Structural differences across regions can clearly produce conflicts about the appropriate monetary response to disturbances. Such conflicts tend to be rare within currency unions, as a common currency generally creates a legal and financial (although not necessarily industrial) structure which is similar across regions. However, such concerns are much more likely to be important in a fledgling currency union of the type proposed in Europe, where a number of countries with relatively diverse financial and legal systems are to be brought together. One example of such structural differences would be the much greater importance of flexible interest rate mortgage loans in the United Kingdom than elsewhere in Europe. Because of this difference in lending practices, the impact on consumers of raising short-term interest rates is much larger in the United Kingdom than in (say) Germany as, in addition to its direct effect on credit conditions, it increases mortgage costs to most home owners. Other structural differences could include divergent relationships between money, wages, prices and unemployment caused by national taxes, labor market structures, or banking systems. Such differences clearly imply that, even when faced by the same situation, the desired monetary response may differ across regions. While a single currency would presumably produce powerful forces toward integrating the financial and legal structures across regional economies, this integration would still take time, and in the interim such structural differences might cause significant disagreements between policy makers.

A similar argument has been made concerning differences in preferences about inflation and monetary policy. Flemming (1971) and Corden (1972) both suggested that differences in policy preferences could make it more difficult to form a currency union, working with a traditional Phillips curve relationship in which there was a long-run trade-off between inflation and unemployment. For such divergences in policy preferences to be a limitation on forming a currency union, such attitudes would need to reflect deep differences about the role of monetary policy held by the public. One could argue, for example, that the attitude of the Bundesbank toward inflation reflects the experience of Germans of ruinous hyperinflation earlier in the century, an experience which most other Europeans did not share. However, if these differences in preferences simply reflect divergent assessments of the costs of inflation across central banks, or disagreements over other such imponderables, then the argument would appear somewhat weaker. Replacing one set of uncertain views about the role of monetary policy with another set of uncertain views is neither clearly beneficial or harmful to the economy.

Recent work on divergent policy preferences has emphasized the role of structural factors in determining an optimum currency area, such as differences in the optimum level of the inflation tax, or the value of a single currency in solving the time inconsistency problem for monetary policy.[21] The time inconsistency problem with regard to monetary policy was outlined in a paper by Robert Barro and David Gordon in 1983.[22] They presented a model in which an unexpected monetary expansion could temporarily drive down the unemployment rate, but could have no effect on its long-term level. A monetary authority which aims to maximize welfare in each period will attempt to use this temporary trade-off to lower the level of unemployment by a surprise expansion of the money supply. As the general public realizes the incentives facing the monetary authority, however, they anticipate this monetary expansion. The result of the policy is higher inflation, with no change in the unemployment rate. This outcome can be improved by imposing a rule to limit the rate of expansion of the money supply, since it generates lower inflation at no cost to unemployment.

Such arguments have been highly influential in monetary policy debates over the last decade and a half, providing the intellectual basis for (among other things) European countries using a peg to the deutsche mark as part of a policy to reduce domestic inflation.[23] The Bundesbank, it was argued, had a successful record of ensuring low inflation. Part of the anti-inflationary reputation could be imported through the use of an exchange rate peg.[24] Such considerations appear to be important for at least one existing currency union, namely the CFA franc zone, where the main benefit to the participants has been the nominal anchor provided by the link with the French franc.[25]

This argument has spilled over into the debate over EMU, where proponents of the single currency have argued that the independence of the new European central bank would provide benefits for the members of EMU by reducing the time inconsistency problem for monetary policy.[26] Clearly, a single currency is one way of obtaining such independence for the monetary authorities. It has the potential advantage that a union-wide monetary authority may find it easier to surmount pressures from sub-union governments, and hence easier to adopt best practices.[27] However, all this has elements of using a sledge hammer to crack a nut. If a government really believes that time inconsistency is a problem for monetary policy, it is difficult to believe that it is necessary to create a European-wide currency to solve the problem. A more direct method is surely to make the existing national central bank independent. (Such an approach appears to have been quite successful in recent years in New Zealand.) Extranational monetary authorities would thus appear to be most important in cases where the institutional framework is particularly weak. The CFA franc zone might well be such a case, although the significantly better inflation rates experienced by the CFA franc zone compared with other African countries appears to have come from the fact that the CFA franc was pegged to the French franc, rather that directly from the existence of the currency union.

Benefits

The smaller literature on the benefits of a currency union focuses on the two major characteristics of money: it is a store of value and a means of transactions.[28] Lower transactions costs provide a number of benefits. Direct savings come from not having to employ people and machines to exchange one type of money to another, freeing resources to be put to more productive uses in the rest of the economy, and from avoiding the associated 'shoe-leather' costs of using these services. Also, if the currency union is also a customs union and goods are allowed to flow freely without customs charges within the currency area, as is generally the case, it is not necessary to have the same number of customs guards monitoring the flow of goods between regions. In addition to these direct benefits, lower transactions costs could have indirect benefits through reducing uncertainties about movements in relative prices, increasing competition between companies, and allowing greater use of economies of scale. The US economy has probably benefitted greatly from its large domestic market, which has allowed industries to specialize and compete while retaining an efficient level of production.

A larger economy may also enhance the usefulness of a currency as a store of value. It is probably no surprise that most international reserves are held in US dollars, or that the relative importance of the yen and deutsche mark have grown in line with the increased economic importance of Japan and Germany, and (in the case of the deutsche mark) moves to limit exchange rate fluctuations within

Europe. A stable store of value benefits domestic consumers through making it easier to plan for the future and through the seigniorage and interest rate benefits generated by a demand for the currency from the rest of the world.

Many of the benefits of money are in the nature of a public good – they rise as the number of participants increase. It is therefore tempting to argue that there will be a general tendency to have currency unions which are too small. Such an argument, however, ignores the fact that the costs of a currency union (caused by a lack of monetary independence) are also often in the nature of a public good. Hence, there is no obvious reason for currency unions to be too large or too small. What it does illustrate, however, is that markets cannot necessarily determine the size of currency unions efficiently.

Finally, there are some interesting incentive issues associated with the benefits of a currency union. In Bayoumi (1994) I analyzed a model in which benefits of a single currency accrue only to participating regions, while the costs affect all countries in the world. This creates the possibility that a region which would prefer that the status quo of freely floating exchange rates was maintained might still have an incentive to join a new currency union which was being formed, as staying out of the union generates more costs than joining it. Another result is that the net benefits of an outside region joining an existing union are generally larger for the entrant than for the existing members. This is because the entrant benefits from lower transactions costs with all regions in the existing union, while the existing members gain only from lower transactions costs with the entrant.

Conclusions

Looking to the future, there are a number of areas where our understanding of currency unions could be extended. First, it would be useful to develop a framework in which the various considerations in the conventional approach to optimum currency areas could be integrated, possibly along the lines suggested in this chapter. A couple of attempts have made a start at such a project by using small general equilibrium models to look at various incentive issues in currency unions, although to make the results tractable these models have been kept fairly simple.[29] A partial equilibrium approach may allow more of the factors discussed in this chapter to be included in a single model, albeit at the cost of generality.

A second area which could be usefully explored further is whether economic integration increases or decreases the benefits of a single currency. There are two views about this interaction. Some argue that lower trade costs will lead to increased regional specialization across industries, thereby making underlying disturbances less symmetric and raising the costs of a currency union. Others argue that greater trade tends to make a currency union easier. For example, increased trade could lower the costs of a single currency by diversifying the demand for products, thereby making the region less susceptible to changes in local income. Chapter 7 provides some new theoretical work on the relationship between economic integration and optimum currency areas.

Another issue is the impact of a currency union on non-exchange rate responses to disturbances. It is often argued that, by ensuring that the exchange rate will not vary in response to disturbances, a single currency may well increase the incentives to use other adjustment mechanisms, such as wage flexibility or labor mobility, in the face of shock. As discussed in the next chapter, empirical work on the relationship between the labor market and the exchange rate regime does tend to indicate that fixed exchange rates are associated with greater wage flexibility. Finally, it is clear that more work could usefully be done on the benefits from a single currency. Some work in this area has already begun. However, the existing models are highly stylized, leaving a wide scope for future endeavors.

Notes

1 The original contribution to this literature was by Mundell (1961). Other early work includes McKinnon (1963) and Kenen (1969). Surveys of the literature include Ishiyama (1975), Tavlas (1993, 1994), and Masson and Taylor (1993).

2 One can distinguish different levels of monetary integration based on considerations such as openness of capital movements and the existence of a single central bank (Corden, 1972; Tavlas, 1994). However, the increasing openness of international capital markets is limiting the feasibility of intermediate solutions. At least one commentator (Eichengreen, 1995) sees the choice of monetary regime as becoming increasingly polarized between floating exchange rates with open international capital markets and currency unions.

3 This can be seen in old treasure troves, which generally contain coins from a number of different places.

4 These paper claims were initially defined in terms of underlying commodities. The pound sterling, for example, was originally a claim on a pound of sterling silver. However, as the paper itself was essentially worthless, the bank had the power to change this rate of exchange.

5 The price of the US dollar was fixed in terms of gold until March 1968. Since the value of many other currencies was fixed against the US dollar, the system had some elements of a commodity standard. Since March 1968, however, no currency has been fixed in terms of gold or silver. Indeed, the Second Amendment to the Articles of Agreement of the International Monetary Fund, which codified the current system of floating exchange rates, explicitly disallows currencies from fixing themselves in terms of gold.

6 For a more formal model of optimum currency areas see Bayoumi (1994).

7 Exceptions include Ishiyama (1975) and Tower and Willett (1976), who both tried to put the theory in a more general context.

8 Although different economic structures, discussed further below, do give one possible avenue for such costs.

9 Note that the size of the underlying shocks is at least as important as their correlations. Work on disturbances often only emphasizes the latter.

10 Existing currency unions can also have significantly different regional disturbances. Consider the United States, the largest currency union in the world in terms of GDP. The constraints of a single monetary policy have generally had least impact on the eastern seaboard and midwest, which dominate the country economically, contain the major financial and political centers, and have relatively similar disturbances. By contrast, the regions producing oil and raw materials in the southwest and Rocky Mountains have been subject to large idiosyncratic disturbances and, particularly in the case of the oil-producing regions, have often been completely out of synchronization with the economic cycle of the rest of the country. This is not to say that these latter regions have not been net beneficiaries of the currency union. However, it is clear that the costs of a single currency have been higher in these areas than in the eastern half of the country.

11 de Grauwe (1992); see also Ricci (1996).

12 Kempa uses a Lucas supply function.

13 Kareken and Wallace (1981) show that the exchange rate is not even well determined in many flexible price models.

14 Kempa (1995) uses the same approach, but eliminates the information advantage of the central bank.

15 Mundell (1961) focused on this issue. Ingram (1962) also discussed capital market integration as a criterion of an optimum currency area.

16 Barro (1974).

17 The problems of reconciling differing preferences for government services across jurisdictions with a federal fiscal system are discussed by Alesina *et al.* (1995).

18 Lucas (1978).

19 McKinnon (1963).

20 See Tavlas (1994) for a fuller discussion of these issues.

21 See Canzoneri and Rogers (1990) for the former, and, for example, Alesina and Grilli (1992, 1993) for the latter.

22 See also Rogoff (1985). It forms part of the more general literature on rules versus discretion (Kyland and Prescott, 1977).

23 Giavazzi and Pagano (1988).

24 Empirical evidence for such credibility effects remains open to debate.

25 Boughton (1993).

26 Alesina and Grilli (1993) and de Grauwe (1992). Winkler (1995) uses this type of model to look at the logic of the Maastricht convergence criteria.

27 Alesina and Grilli (1993).

28 Formal models of the benefits of money are still in their infancy. Examples include Casella (1992) and Dowd and Greenway (1993).

29 Bayoumi (1994) and Ricci (1996).

6 Empirical work on optimum currency areas

Empirical work on optimum currency areas is considerably younger than its theoretical counterpart. Indeed, almost all the empirical studies have been written since the late 1980s. This difference in timing reflects events in the wider world. While theoretical interest in the issue was generated by the controversy about the relative merits of fixed and floating exchange rates, there was little change or prospect of change in the existing set of currency unions between the early 1960s and the mid-1980s – the main exceptions being newly independent states created by the decline of colonial rule. The question of whether the existing set of currency unions was appropriate or not was therefore regarded as being of primarily theoretical interest.[1]

Recent events, including the break-up of currency unions in the former Soviet Union, Yugoslavia, Czechoslovakia, and regional separatist movements in industrial countries, such as the Parti Quebequois in Canada and the Lombardy League in northern Italy, have ignited the issue of whether the existing set of currencies are beneficial. More generally, at least one commentator has argued that, with international capital markets becoming increasingly open, countries may be faced with a stark choice between joining a currency union with other countries or accepting a floating exchange rate against them.[2]

The driving force behind recent empirical work on optimum currency areas, however, comes from a specific potential agglomeration of currencies, in the form of plans for EMU in western Europe. Initial plans for such an undertaking were provided by the Delors Committee (1989), and a detailed path to such a monetary union was laid out in 1992 in the Maastricht treaty signed by the heads of state of the European Community (EC). As the prospects of a single currency for large parts of western Europe have moved forward, so has academic work on the suitability of western Europe for such an experiment.

Consequently, recent empirical work on currency unions has focused very largely on western Europe, although there has also been a considerable amount of EMU-inspired research on behavior within existing currency unions, in particular the United States.[3] This work has been geared to providing a guide as to what changes in behavior might occur within Europe as a result of adopting a single currency. It has also, incidentally, produced a better understanding of the workings of existing currency unions.

The structure of this chapter will mirror that of the previous chapter, on the theory of optimum currency areas. It starts with a review of work on the size and correlation of disturbances across regions and countries. Next comes a discussion of evidence on mechanisms which can substitute for the exchange rate in adjustment (such as labor mobility), followed by a review of work on factors which might inhibit the value of the exchange rate as a method of adjustment (such as openness to trade), and on reasons why desired monetary responses to disturbances might vary with economic structure. Next comes a review of work on the benefits of a single currency. The chapter concludes with a discussion of results from international macroeconomic models and some more general observations about the state of the existing literature and potential for future development.

Although the chapter inevitably focuses largely on evidence on western Europe, it is not intended to be an assessment of prospects for EMU.[4] Rather, the discussion focuses on what this work can tell us about currency unions in general. For this reason, the chapter reviews the more important aspects of each contribution, rather than attempting a comprehensive review of all results.[5]

Underlying disturbances

One of the first empirical papers to consider the nature of underlying disturbances in the context of a currency union was a wide-ranging discussion of prospects for EMU by Cohen and Wyplosz (1989). Using data on real output, prices, wages, and the current account (as a ratio to GDP) in France and Germany, they compared the variation of the sum and differences of these variables across the two countries. The logic of the test was that if countries behave similarly, then the variation of the sum of the variables will be much larger than that of the difference. By contrast, if behavior was very different the variability of the difference should rise and that of the sum should fall. They found that disturbances in France and Germany were similar, both absolutely and relative to disturbances in France and Germany (combined) compared with the United States. Weber (1990) extended the analysis by looking at behavior across the seven existing members of the ERM (France, Germany, Italy, the Netherlands, Belgium, Denmark, and Ireland) and a wider range of variables. He concluded that disturbances within the region were similar, but that for real wages this was true only between Germany and its smaller immediate neighbors (the Netherlands, Belgium, and Denmark), making this subgroup better candidates for EMU than the region as a whole.

A potential problem with using data on (say) real GDP to measure underlying real disturbances is that changes in real GDP reflect both the underlying disturbances and the response of the economy to these disturbances. Corporale (1993) used the residuals from autoregressions on real output to identify the underlying disturbances; however, the resulting correlations were not very intuitive. Bayoumi and Eichengreen (1993a) used structural VARs, in which data on real output and prices were used to identify underlying aggregate demand and supply disturbances, and responses to these disturbances, across the 12 existing members of the EC (as the EU was then called) and across eight regions of the United States.[6]

The results indicated that the EC was divided into a core of countries with highly correlated shocks, made up of Germany and its immediate neighbors (France, the Netherlands, Belgium, and Denmark) and a periphery of regions whose disturbances were larger and more idiosyncratic. Only if the European analysis was limited to these core countries were the size and coherence of the disturbances across the EC similar to those across the United States.[7] We also found that the adjustment to disturbances was generally faster for US regions than EC countries, indicating that the United States had a more flexible economic structure than the EC. Our conclusion was that the core countries of the EC appeared to be better designed for a currency union than the EC as a whole. In a subsequent paper we extended the analysis to the main six countries which were then members of the European Free Trade Association (EFTA), Austria, Switzerland, Sweden, Norway, Finland, and Iceland.[8] The results indicated that Austria, Sweden, and Switzerland were part of a European core, and Norway, Finland, and Iceland were part of the periphery. This suggests that the recent expansion of the EU (as the EC renamed itself) to include

Table 6.1 Correlations of estimated aggregate supply disturbances in western Europe, 1963–90

	Ger-many	France	Nether-lands	Bel-gium	Den-mark	Aus-tria	Switzer-land	Italy	UK	Spain	Port-ugal	Ire-land	Sweden	Nor-way
France	**0.52**													
Netherlands	**0.54**	0.36												
Belgium	**0.62**	**0.40**	**0.56**											
Denmark	**0.68**	**0.54**	**0.56**	**0.37**										
Austria	**0.41**	0.28	**0.38**	**0.47**	**0.49**									
Switzerland	**0.38**	0.25	**0.58**	**0.47**	0.36	**0.39**								
Italy	0.21	0.28	**0.39**	-0.00	0.15	0.06	-0.04							
UK	0.12	0.12	0.13	0.12	-0.05	-0.25	0.16	0.28						
Spain	0.33	0.21	0.17	0.23	0.22	0.25	0.07	0.20	0.01					
Portugal	0.21	0.33	0.11	**0.40**	-0.04	-0.03	0.13	0.22	0.27	**0.51**				
Ireland	-0.00	-0.21	0.11	-0.02	-0.32	0.08	0.08	0.14	0.05	-0.15	0.01			
Sweden	0.31	0.30	**0.43**	0.06	0.35	0.01	**0.44**	**0.46**	**0.41**	0.20	**0.39**	0.10		
Norway	-0.27	-0.11	-0.39	-0.26	-0.37	-0.21	-0.18	0.01	0.27	-0.09	0.26	0.08	0.10	
Finland	0.22	0.12	-0.25	0.06	0.30	0.11	0.06	-0.32	-0.04	0.07	-0.13	-0.23	-0.10	-0.08

Bold figures are significantly different from zero at the 5 percent level.
Source: Bayoumi and Eichengreen (1994b).

Table 6.2 Correlations of estimated aggregate supply disturbances in the United States, 1963–86

	New England	Mid-east	Great Lakes	Plains	Far west	South-east
Mid-east	**0.86**					
Great Lakes	**0.77**	**0.81**				
Plains	**0.44**	**0.67**	**0.66**			
Far west	**0.62**	**0.52**	**0.65**	**0.49**		
Southeast	0.34	0.30	**0.46**	**0.43**	0.32	
West	0.07	-0.18	-0.11	-0.33	-0.66	0.26

Bold figures are significantly different from zero at the 5 percent level.
Source: Bayoumi and Eichengreen (1994b).

Austria, Sweden, and Finland should not pose any significant new problems for EMU.

A sense of these results can be obtained from Tables 6.1 and 6.2. Table 6.1 shows the correlation matrix between estimated underlying aggregate supply disturbances for western Europe, with values which are significant at the 5 percent level appearing in bold type. Germany, France, the Netherlands, Denmark, Austria, and Switzerland clearly have more highly correlated disturbances than do the rest of Europe. Table 6.2 reports similar calculations across seven US regions. The core in this case includes all the regions except the west, largely a producer of raw materials, and, possibly, the southeast.

We also extended our work outside Europe to look at behavior between regions within NAFTA (Canada, the United States, and Mexico) and across western Europe, the Americas and east Asia, while Bayoumi and Ostry (1995) looked at similar issues with respect to Africa. The results for the members of NAFTA indicated that North America splits into two distinct regions, each with relatively coherent underlying disturbances: the predominantly industrial eastern half of the continent, made up of the northeast seaboard, southeast, and midwest regions in the United States, plus California in the west; and the western half producing raw materials, comprising western Canada, the northwest and southwest of the United States (excluding California), and Mexico.[9] This division suggests that North America is not well suited for a single currency. Indeed, from an optimum currency area perspective, the logical division of North America is not the north–south boundaries which have actually come into place between Canada, the United States, and Mexico, but an east–west division of the type suggested by Mundell (1961).

The results for western Europe, the Americas and east Asia confirmed the earlier results regarding the core–periphery distinction in western Europe and the unsuitability of North America as currently constituted for closer monetary ties.[10] In east Asia, two groups of countries were found to have similar disturbances, namely Japan, Korea, and Taiwan, and Hong Kong, Indonesia, Malaysia, Singapore, and (possibly) Thailand, suggesting that these regions may be good candidates for closer monetary ties over the foreseeable future. However, Australia and New Zealand were found to have relatively diverse disturbances. As in the case of the United States and Canada, this may help explain the lack of interest in closer monetary ties between these nations. Similarly, there was little evidence of groups of countries in South America or in Africa which had sufficiently similar disturbances to make them reasonable candidates for closer monetary cooperation.

A number of works have extended the analysis of disturbances in western Europe. For example, Funke (1995), using updated data, found significantly lower correlations between other EU core countries and Germany than our earlier work, most notably for France, a result he attributes to the impact of German unification.[11] This illustrates how a large asymmetric disturbance – in this case German unification – can influence the empirical results. He also reports correlations across 11 west German *Länder*, and finds them to be similar in many respects to those we obtained for the United States. Other researchers, such as Chamie *et al.* (1994) and Erkel-Rousse and Melitz (1995), also find smaller cores than we did. Both papers extended the number of equations in the VAR so as to differentiate types of aggregate demand shocks. Given the theoretical differences in the impact of real and monetary disturbances implied by the Mundell–Flemming open economy framework, this differentiation could clearly be a useful guide to how the composition of differing types of shocks could impact a monetary union, although this issue is not fully pursued in the papers.

Using a slightly different approach, de Grauwe and Vanhaverbeke (1992) used regional data to look at disturbances within and between European countries. They found that the variance of the growth of output and employment between regions within EU countries is at least as large as, if not larger than, that between EU countries (however, they did not look at correlations across regions of different nations). They also found that labor mobility is a more important equilibrating force within countries than between them, while exchange rate flexibility has the opposite characteristic. They point to an optimistic and a pessimistic interpretation of these results. The optimistic view is that asymmetric disturbances are currently small within Europe, and that the process of integration is likely to make them smaller, implying very limited adjustment costs with EMU. The pessimistic view is that greater integration will lead to regional concentration and agglomeration effects, which will increase the strain on non-exchange rate methods of adjustment. They note that evidence of concentration from the United States would tend to support the more pessimistic interpretation.[12]

Finally, Ghosh and Wolf (1994) provide a very general method of looking at the costs of asymmetric disturbances across countries using a generic algorithm, which they apply to changes in real output, rather than trying to identify underlying disturbances. Under this approach, costs are calculated across all possible combinations of countries (or regions), and the optimum combinations of countries are calculated given either an assumed level of benefits which a currency union provides or (more simply) by how many currency unions are assumed to exist within the area. This approach is clearly very general, and could be extended in several directions. At the same time, it should be noted that the currency unions actually calculated by Ghosh and Wolf do not always appear particularly intuitive.

Overall, the empirical analysis of the size and correlation of underlying disturbances confirms several predictions of the optimum currency literature. Disturbances within both the United States and the former West Germany appear to be highly correlated, implying relatively small asymmetric disturbances across regions within countries. Some core parts of western Europe also experience relatively correlated disturbances, which may well explain the interest in monetary union in this part of the world. By contrast, the low correlation of disturbances between the United States as a whole and Canada as a whole, and between Australia and New Zealand, appear consistent with the lack of enthusiasm for a single currency in these parts of the world. Finally, the evidence appears to indicate that short-term disturbances within countries are of a similar size to those between countries.

Nonmonetary response mechanisms

There has also been an expanding literature on non-exchange rate adjustment mechanisms within and across countries. The level of relative price variability across regions within currency unions has been studied by a number of authors.[13] Most have concluded that relative price variability is significantly smaller within currency unions than across European countries. This implies that EMU could reduce the ability of European countries to use relative prices to respond to economic disturbances. Poloz (1990), however, found that relative price variability across Canadian provinces is similar to that between France, the United Kingdom, Italy, and Germany, implying a more favorable view of the potential role for relative price variability in EMU.

An alternative approach has been to use estimated wage equations to look at the role of relative prices in adjustment. Bini-Smaghi and Vori (1993) report results from a number of such exercises which indicate that real wage rigidity is higher in the EU than in the United States and Japan. They argue that this implies that nominal variables (including the exchange rate) are relatively ineffective instruments in Europe, and hence that the loss of the exchange rate would not have large costs.[14] Clearly, rigidities in relative prices, such as real wages, cannot be alleviated by nominal policies. However, as these real rigidities are only partial, it is not clear that this implies that the exchange rate should not be used as a policy tool.

Wage behavior may also depend upon the exchange rate regime. More flexible exchange rates may reduce the need to use wages to adjust to shocks, and hence lower labor market flexibility. The literature on the interaction between labor markets and the exchange rate regime is limited and inconclusive. Alogoskoufis and Smith (1991) and Eichengreen (1993) provide historical evidence that wage flexibility rises with fixed exchange rates. Blanchard and Muet (1993), however, detect little sign that French wage behavior changed as the government's commitment to its ERM exchange rate peg hardened over the 1980s and early 1990s. Finally, Anderton and Barrell (1993) report some evidence of increasing wage flexibility in Italy over the period of that country's ERM membership.

Labor mobility has also been an important topic in the discussion of adjustment mechanisms other than the exchange rate. This reflects the importance that Mundell gave to factor mobility, together with empirical evidence that labor market adjustment is an important means of adjustment within the United States. More specifically, Blanchard and Katz (1992) wrote a highly influential paper looking at the role of wage flexibility and labor migration in restoring labor market equilibrium across US states. They found that after a region experienced (say) a negative employment disturbance, the rise in unemployment produced only a small fall in local wage levels. Rather, they found labor migration to be the major force in restoring labor market equilibrium, with workers moving out of regions where employment prospects at existing wages were declining and moving into regions with expanding employment opportunities. Comparisons of labor markets in the EU have generally found that labor markets there are significantly less flexible than those in the United States, and that migration between EU countries is smaller than that within those countries, probably by an order of magnitude, presumably reflecting deep cultural and linguistic differences across member countries.[15] In particular, Decressin and Fatas (1995) provide an analysis of European labor market adjustment similar to that used by Blanchard and Katz (1992) for the United States. They find that for Europe the main equilibrating factor for labor markets is changes in the participation rate rather than migration. To the extent that these changes in the participation rate reflect an inability to find jobs, this would tend to indicate that Europe is less well designed for a single currency than the United States.

Overall, the evidence would appear to indicate that labor mobility is an important nonmonetary adjustment mechanism within the US currency union, justifying the importance given to factor mobility as a characteristic of an optimum currency area by Mundell. On the other hand, it also appears that labor mobility is higher within the United States than many other currency unions. Hence, while high labor mobility may provide significant benefits for a currency union, it may not be a necessity.

There are by now several empirical studies of the role of federal fiscal policy in insuring regional incomes, particularly federal policy within the United States. An early contribution was the 1977 Mac-Dougall report on the role of public finances in European integration, which concluded that central government fiscal flows were an important offset to interregional income disturbances, reducing such changes by about 40 percent. This figure was broadly confirmed in a more recent paper by Sala-i-Martin and Sachs (1992), in a study focusing on the United States. These results, however, were questioned

by von Hagen (1992), who found a considerably smaller federal
income tax offset in the United States (about 10 percent of income
differentials) using a similar econometric methodology, and concluded
that such fiscal insurance is therefore not important for a successful
monetary union. Subsequent work, however, has tended to support the
original higher estimates of the fiscal offset. In particular, Goodhart
and Smith (1993), in a paper which contains both new econometric
estimates for the United States, Canada, and the United Kingdom, and
an extended discussion of earlier results, conclude 'Our reworking of
von Hagen's exercise has persuaded us that existing federal fiscal
systems (e.g. the United States) do provide a worthwhile element of
such [income] stabilization'.[16]

Bayoumi and Masson (1995) also conclude that federal fiscal
payments provide a significant level of stabilization in both the United
States and Canada. Our estimates of the size of federal automatic
stabilizers for both countries, together with the contribution from
differing elements of the fiscal system (taxes, transfers, and federal
grants to lower levels of government), are reported in Table 6.3. A
feature of Table 6.3 is the wide variation in the importance of different
types of fiscal instrument across the two fiscal systems, and the lower
level of stabilization provided by the Canadian federal government
compared with that in the United States. These results indicate that the
size of automatic stabilizers can vary significantly across currency
unions, presumably reflecting political preferences. Even in Canada,
however, the fiscal offset from the federal government to changes in
local income is large, almost 20 cents in the dollar. We also extended
the analysis to look at levels of automatic stabilizers provided by five
European countries. These results, also reported in Table 6.3, show
that national governments in Europe provided a level of automatic
stabilizers to their own countries which is very similar to that provided
by the federal government across regions within the United States.

More recent work by us provides evidence that the level of government at which the fiscal stabilizers operate may also be important.[17] As
discussed in the previous chapter, stabilization will tend to be more
effective when it is provided across the entire currency union, as such
a centralized fiscal system can insure against idiosyncratic shocks
across regions within the union. Our results indicate that fiscal deficits
run by provincial governments within Canada may have only one-third
to one-half the impact on private consumption of federal deficits in
that province, which are offset by federal surpluses elsewhere within

Table 6.3   The size of automatic stabilizers (percent offset to a change in income)

	United States	Canada	Five European countries
Taxes	8.6	3.4	10.4
Transfers	14.4	10.9	20.4
Grants to lower levels of government	7.2	3.1	–
Total	30.2	17.4	30.8

Notes: Taxes include social insurance payments.
Source: Bayoumi and Masson (1995).

Canada (changes in the federal deficit at the national level have the same impact as provincial government deficits at the provincial level).[18] This suggests that there is a significant cost to operating automatic stabilizers at a decentralized level.

Income insurance can also be achieved through private capital markets. Atkeson and Bayoumi (1993) looked at the importance of such flows within the United States. They estimated the relative importance of three types of investment flows into individual states: those that offset fluctuations in labor income, those that correspond to changes in aggregate US behavior, and those correlated with local returns on capital. We concluded that private capital markets provided very little direct offset to fluctuations in labor income (about 1 cent in the dollar). However, these private capital flows were also largely unrelated to local returns to capital. Instead, they mainly reflected national developments. Since such flows provide a significant proportion of overall personal income, this implies that private capital markets reduce fluctuations in personal income largely through their lack of correlation with the return on local capital. The paper did not provide an estimate of the size of this effect. However, Asdrubali *et al.* (1996) estimate that private capital markets reduce income fluctuations by 40 percent. Note, however, that part of this may be due to dividend smoothing by firms. Hence, aggregate local incomes may be smoothed less than personal local incomes.

Effectiveness of the exchange rate

Empirical work on mechanisms which change the effectiveness of the
real exchange rate has gone in several directions. One has been to
focus on the McKinnon criterion of openness to trade by looking at
trade within and between various blocs of countries.[19] Data for merchandise trade (direction-of-trade figures for services are difficult to
obtain) indicate that in 1990 western Europe (EC and EFTA combined) and North America (the United States, Canada, and Mexico)
were relatively closed to trade with the rest of the world, in that such
trade (defined as the sum of exports and imports) made up only
between 10 and 15 percent of GDP, while it comprised 20 percent of
GDP in 11 east Asian and Pacific countries.[20] By contrast, intra-
regional trade represented 33 percent of GDP in western Europe, and
even more in many of the smaller and more highly integrated economies such as Belgium and the Netherlands. Intra-regional trade is also
over 30 percent of GDP for Canada in North America, and Hong
Kong, Singapore, Malaysia, Thailand, and Taiwan in east Asia.

The relatively high ratios of intra-regional trade in Europe may
explain the interest shown in exchange rate stabilization in this region,
as illustrated by the ERM, and of the policy of the Canadian government to limited exchange rate volatility between Canadian and US
dollars, and the similar low volatility between the Swiss franc and
deutsche mark.[21] Such observations would tend to confirm that bilateral trade promotes exchange rate stability. More direct evidence
that exchange rate variability is indeed connected with several variables of the optimum currency area type, including bilateral trade, is
provided in Bayoumi and Eichengreen (1997).

Another way of gauging the potential importance of openness is to
compare levels of trade across countries with trade within them.
Unfortunately, because countries are also generally customs unions,
such information is rarely available. An exception is Canada, where
levels of internal and external trade across provinces for 1989 are
reported by Messinger (1993). Table 6.4 reports some measures of
intra-Canadian and extra-Canadian openness derived from the data.
Internal trade in goods and services turns out to be slightly smaller
than trade with the rest of the world, with the internal trade ratio (of
exports plus imports) being 45 percent of GDP and the external
being 50 percent of GDP. When the internal trade figures are limited
only to goods, which makes them more comparable to the data on

Table 6.4   Canadian provincial trade ratios, 1989 (percent of GDP)

	Interprovincial trade in goods	Interprovincial trade in goods and services	International trade in goods and services
Newfoundland	29.5	53.7	47.5
Prince Edward Island	49.0	81.5	25.7
Nova Scotia	37.1	63.4	40.4
New Brunswick	47.2	71.3	53.4
Quebec	29.3	45.3	43.5
Ontario	22.5	36.8	58.4
Manitoba	36.6	61.6	34.8
Saskatchewan	39.5	63.9	40.2
Alberta	36.2	60.1	40.5
British Columbia	19.4	37.9	46.1
Yukon and Northwest Territories	41.9	81.8	42.5
Canada	27.2	44.8	49.5

The underlying data come from Messinger (1993) and the Canadian *Provincial National Accounts*.

merchandise trade quoted above, the level of interprovincial trade is only 27 percent of GDP, over 5 percent lower than the ratio between the 18 members of the EC and EFTA in 1990.

There are some reasons for believing that Canada may have somewhat lower internal trade ratios than many other countries. The sheer size and proximity of the US economy encourages external trade (particularly as many of the natural trade routes in North America run north–south rather than east–west), as does the loose nature of the federation, which allows provinces to erect barriers to interprovincial trade. Also, output in the west is heavily concentrated in the production of raw materials, which may have a higher propensity to be exported to the rest of the world. On the other hand, trade within Canada does appear to be quite highly integrated. McCallum (1995), using a gravity trade model, concludes that intra-Canadian trade is over 20 times higher than would be expected given the level of trade between Canada and the United States. In any case, it is striking that interprovincial trade of goods in Canada, a smoothly functioning currency union, has a slightly lower ratio to GDP than the existing level of interregional trade in the EC.

A separate literature has developed around the issue of how a single currency might affect regional specialization of output. Krugman (1993), Bini-Smaghi and Vori (1993) and Masson and Taylor (1993) all note that manufacturing production is much more geographically concentrated within the United States than within the EU, which implies that a single currency might be easier to implement in Europe. However, Krugman also argues that this difference reflects the existence of the US currency and customs union, and that a single currency in Europe could make production more geographically specialized and hence a single currency more difficult to maintain.[22] Bayoumi and Prasad (1995) look at sectoral diversification across the whole of GDP, rather than manufacturing, for eight European countries and eight regions of the United States. Our results indicate that the United States is more geographically diversified in manufacturing and primary goods, but is less diversified in other sectors. We infer that, while manufacturing may become more specialized owing to a single currency, the unification of regulations and rules implied by a single currency may cause many other sectors of the economy to become less diversified.

A key issue in the discussion of the importance of sectoral diversification is the source of underlying regional disturbances. If such disturbances are generally region-specific, reflecting local conditions, then the industrial structure would be largely irrelevant to the nature of the regional disturbances. If, on the other hand, disturbances are primarily industry-specific, reflecting technological changes and the like, industrial structure would clearly matter. Industry-specific disturbances are more likely to result in asymmetric disturbances across regions which are highly specialized than ones which are more diversified.

Techniques to decompose fluctuations in output (and employment) into their industry-specific and region-specific components had already been developed as part of the investigation of the nature of the business cycle.[23] Bini-Smaghi and Vori (1993) used such a decomposition to look at the nature of the underlying disturbances to manufacturing production across European countries and regions of the United States. They concluded that region-specific disturbances were relatively unimportant in Europe, particularly for the original six members of the EC, implying that the exchange rate might not be such a useful method of adjustment to disturbances in this region. More recently, Bayoumi and Prasad (1995) returned to this issue, looking at output across all industries. We too found that region-specific disturbances were relatively unimportant for manufacturing industry. However, for the economy as a whole we found that region-specific disturbances were almost as important as industry-specific disturbances in both Europe and the United States, and that aggregate disturbances, affecting all regions and industries, were slightly more important than either.

Ghosh and Wolf (1996) looked at shocks across the United States utilizing a particularly narrow definition of industries. Using a number of different techniques they concluded that industry-specific shocks tend to dominate region-specific ones at this level of disaggregation. They also found, however, that this result tended to change as the number of identified industries was reduced by amalgamation. This raises the issue of aggregation. When industries are defined sufficiently finely, the distinction between region-specific and industry-specific disturbances may become blurred. To take a concrete example, almost all US cars are made in the midwest, so that an industry-specific shock to the car industry is also, in effect, a regional shock.

While the relative importance of industry-specific and region-specific shocks, and the inference from such results, is thus open to some debate, the most important conclusion from the point of view of optimum currency areas is that most analyses of the United States and European countries find that the behavior of these disturbances is similar. Hence, differences in types of underlying disturbance do not appear to be major obstacles to the formation of a currency union, at least in western Europe. It may also imply that the existence of a currency union does not affect the incidence of such disturbances to any large extent.

Policy conflicts

Empirical work on the impact of structural differences across economies on the desired path for monetary policy has moved in two main directions. The first is to look at differences in the transmission mechanisms of monetary policy. Some aggregate results on western European on labor markets – wage and price adjustment and labor migration – have already been discussed. De Grauwe and Vanhaverbeke (1992) also report differences in labor market behavior across countries. They find that labor markets in northern Europe are considerably more flexible than their southern counterparts. Although not explored in the paper, such differences could lead to divergent monetary priorities.

A related issue is the degree to which differences in financial markets affect the transmission of monetary policy. A clear distinction is often made between the so-called 'Anglo-Saxon' financial systems (such as those in the United States, the United Kingdom, Australia, and Canada), where financing of industry is highly dependent upon organized markets, and financial systems where banks have a more important role in financing industry (for example, those in Germany and France). There is also the issue of home ownership. Here there is a difference between the United Kingdom, which has a large number of home owners with adjustable-rate loans, and other developed countries, where home loans are either less prevalent or are generally made at a fixed rate of interest. Because of the nature of the home loans, changes in short-term interest rates have more significant consequences for many people's disposable income in the United Kingdom than elsewhere, thereby making changes in short-term interest rates more politically and economically sensitive than in other countries. Most comparisons between differing financial systems have often been primarily anecdotal. Recent work at the Bank for International Settlements, however, has begun to measure these differences more systematically.[24]

The other major issue associated with the conduct of monetary policy has been the effectiveness of differing institutional arrangements in achieving low inflation. Many countries in Europe chose to use an exchange rate peg against the deutsche mark in the ERM as the principle means of achieving lower inflation rates over the late 1980s. One of the reasons for using the exchange rate peg was to gain some of the inflation credibility of the Bundesbank, thereby enhancing the credibility of the policy and, it was hoped, lowering output costs of reducing inflation. The empirical literature remains somewhat divided on the existence of such 'credibility' effects, which probably indicates that, even if they did exist, their impact was not particularly large. Apparently, credibility has to be earned, not borrowed.

Differences in institutional arrangements for monetary policy, however, do appear to affect long-term outcomes. There is now reasonably strong empirical evidence that independent central banks have been associated with lower levels of inflation, and without any clear loss in terms of the stability of output, which has led to a fairly general preference for independent central banks by economists.[25] Since the proposed central bank in Europe will be highly independent, this change in monetary arrangements has been identified by some authors as one of the benefits of EMU. Clearly, any transnational institution will tend to be more independent of political forces than national ones, just as independent central banks tend to be more common in federal states such as the United States and Germany than in unitary ones. On the other hand, even a unitary government can provide for an independent central bank, as has occurred recently in New Zealand. Overall, therefore, I remain unconvinced that this is a discussion about optimum currency areas, as opposed to one about specific circumstances in the EU.

Benefits

Like its theoretical counterpart, the empirical literature on the benefits of a single currency is considerably smaller than the literature on the costs. Comprehensive estimates for western Europe are given by the Commission of the European Communities (1990), which looked at the benefits of eliminating transactions and customs costs, from lower exchange rate uncertainty, from greater efficiency of firms due to more integrated goods markets, and from lower costs of capital due to deeper and more liquid financial markets.

The benefits of eliminating transactions costs in western Europe are estimated to be of the order of 0.4 percent of GDP for the region as a whole, although rising to 1 percent of GDP for some of the smaller economies. These relatively modest totals presumably reflect, in part, the relatively sophisticated financial system in this part of the world. They may also understate the benefits from cross-border shopping and the like, which are not undertaken owing to the difficulties and costs involved in such transactions.[26] Even when all these factors are taken into account, however, the benefits from this source appear unlikely to be substantial.

Eliminating exchange rate variability may also provide greater incentives to trade and invest across borders. As discussed earlier, the elimination of national currencies appears likely to reduce relative price volatility across regions. There is now an extensive empirical literature on the link between exchange rate volatility and trade, with most investigators finding that the effect of exchange rate volatility on trade is small, insignificant, or both.[27] Similar results are found in the much smaller literature on the connection between investment and exchange rate variability.[28] On the other hand, empirical work consistently finds that persistent real exchange rate movements affect trade volumes, implying that more persistent movements in exchange rates which are not connected with fundamentals do disrupt trade. Indeed, such exchange rate misalignments are one of the major concerns with respect to floating exchange rates.[29] Clearly, eliminating the exchange rate uncertainty completely through a single currency, and the institutional and legal changes associated with such a step, might indeed generate a larger expansion of trade than implied by the literature on exchange rate volatility. The results by McCallum (1995), indicating that trade within Canada is 20 times higher than would be expected given trade with the United States, illustrate the point.[30]

The largest benefits estimated by the Commission are associated with the increased productivity caused by greater economic integration and economies of scale. They estimate these gains to be considerable, raising growth by 0.7 percent per annum for the first 10 years and 0.25 percent thereafter. They also estimate that the gains from lower costs of capital caused by the expanded size of financial markets could be substantial – of the order of 5–10 percent of income in the long-run – based largely on earlier analysis by Baldwin (1989).

These results illustrate a general characteristic of estimates of economic benefits from policy changes, namely that they are highly dependent upon the assumptions made about economies of scale. When computational general equilibrium (CGE) models are used to calculate the benefits of policy changes, such as the lowering of international tariffs, the results depend crucially upon the assumptions made about the production technology. When the models assume perfect competition and constant returns to scale, the benefits are in almost all cases relatively small. This is because the gains are limited to marginal benefits as inputs are reallocated across industries, and the sum of such Harberger triangles rarely amounts to very much.[31] By contrast, if economies of scale (or increases in X-efficiency through greater competition) are included, the benefits can be much larger, as higher productivity directly boosts output, and hence welfare, rather than providing gains only in comparison with the next best use.

As very little is known about the empirical effect of economies of scale and increased competition on output, and these factors potentially account for the major part of any benefits of a single currency, it follows that almost equally little is known about these benefits, either in Europe or any anywhere else in the world. (It is scant consolation that this is also true of many other economic questions.)

One last point may be worth making before leaving the issue of measuring the benefits of a single currency. If the benefits through economies of scale and X-efficiency are indeed significant, this may well imply considerable changes in economic structure. Exploiting economies of scale, for example, may imply greater geographical concentration of industry, while increases in productivity through competition could well be accompanied by significant reductions in employment. While clearly producing long-term benefits, the economic dislocation created by such changes also generates short-term economic costs. Experiences with supply-side reforms in countries such as New Zealand and the United Kingdom indicate that these dislocation costs can be both significant and protracted.

Evidence from large models

Up to this point, the discussion has involved explicit consideration of a single aspect of the theory of optimum currency areas, such as the role of labor mobility in adjustment. An alterative approach is to use international macroeconomic models to look at the overall consequences of EMU. This is done by running stochastic simulations, in which the model is rerun with realistic disturbances added so as to estimate the consequences of different policy rules, such as fixed monetary targets and EMU, on the variability of output and inflation. The results are mixed, with EMU being superior in some cases and inferior in others.[32]

That a fixed exchange rate system can lower the variance of output compared with a floating exchange rate system serves as a useful reminder that in a world of second best (where other market inefficiencies exist), exchange rate flexibility is not always beneficial. One of the implicit assumptions in the optimum currency area literature is that exchange rate flexibility is useful as it can reduce the impact of real disturbances on the economy. In a world with sticky wages, however, exchange rate overshooting can induce its own variability in the real economy, particularly if it is assumed that floating exchange rate systems contain some 'excess volatility' – that is, variation which is not related to fundamentals. These results, therefore, weaken one of the fundamental assumptions in much of the theoretical literature. The results from large models may, however, be of slightly less interest than they first appear. The simulations compare the results running different mechanistic monetary rules, such as a fixed level of money supply or a fixed exchange rate regime. As such they do not have a lot to say about some of the major costs or benefits of a single currency. On the cost side, the important feature about a single currency is less that it enforces a fixed exchange rate across currencies than that the rule cannot be broken. It may be true that a fixed exchange rate is superior in response to some types of disturbance, and a floating exchange rate in others. If one has a single currency, however, one does not have the alternative of switching between options in the way that a national currency allows. At the same time, the simulations are essentially silent about the benefits of a single currency in terms of lower transactions costs, expanded trade, and greater competition. The existing literature would therefore appear to have more to say about alternative exchange rate systems than about the benefits and costs of monetary union.

Conclusions

As with any empirical literature, the work on optimum currency areas has both strengths and weaknesses. On the positive side, it appears that some relatively successful techniques have been developed for measuring the size and correlation of underlying disturbances across regions. In addition, there is now a much fuller understanding of the role of labor mobility in restoring equilibrium within existing currency unions. Despite some continuing controversies, much has also been learned about issues such as the level of insurance provided by federal tax systems. More generally, the criteria identified in the theoretical literature on optimum currency areas – asymmetric shocks, openness, labor mobility – do indeed appear to matter in actual currency unions. An interesting extension of the empirical work on optimum currency areas would be to see how well these considerations predict the behavior of exchange rates across countries. Limiting exchange rate volatility with other countries involves some loss of monetary autonomy, and is therefore likely to involve similar considerations as the choice of whether to participate in a currency union.[33]

What is currently most noticeably lacking from the literature on the potential costs of a currency union is a way of adding these disparate factors together in order to come up with an estimate of overall cost, or with an analysis of which sectors of society will be most affected. Carefully constructed simulations using macroeconomic or computational equilibrium models might provide a way of doing this.

By contrast, the literature on the benefits of a currency union has the opposite characteristic. There have been a number of exercises which have attempted to put a relatively precise value on the potential benefits of a currency union, at least in Europe. The problem is that the lion's share of such benefits come from factors such as economies of scale, whose actual value is highly uncertain. In sum, the menu is fairly complete, but the assessment of the relative importance of different factors is still lacking.

Notes

1 Indeed, Ishiyama (1975, p. 378) described the optimum currency literature as 'primarily a scholastic discussion which contributes little to the practical problems of exchange rate policy and monetary reform.'
2 Eichengreen (1995).
3 The United States is an obvious country to use in looking at the potential success of a single European currency, as it is an existing currency union which is similar to the EC/EU in population and economic size.
4 Surveys of work on EMU include Bean (1992) and Eichengreen (1992c).
5 For example, two papers in the bibliography simply have the title 'Is Europe an Optimum Currency Area?' (de Grauwe and Vanhaverbeke, 1992; Coporale, 1993).
6 The structural VAR methodology was first suggested by Blanchard and Quah (1989).
7 The United States also had a core and periphery; however, the periphery was relatively small, comprising the regions producing raw materials in the southwest and Rocky Mountains, and both the core and periphery generally showed more coherence than their equivalents in the EC.
8 Bayoumi and Eichengreen (1993b).
9 Bayoumi and Eichengreen (1994a).
10 Bayoumi and Eichengreen (1994b).
11 Bayoumi and Eichengreen (1996) confirm this analysis, and also find that German unification did not significantly affect correlations between other members of the core and periphery.

12 See Krugman (1991a) for evidence on concentration of industrial production in the United States.
13 Eichengreen (1990), de Grauwe and Vanhaverbeke (1992), Poloz (1990), and Bayoumi and Thomas (1995).
14 See also Buiter (1995).
15 See, for example, Eichengreen (1990, 1992b), de Grauwe and Vanhaverbeke (1992), and Decressin and Fatas (1995).
16 Goodhart and Smith (1993, p. 437).
17 Bayoumi and Masson (1996).
18 Bernheim (1987), in a survey of the literature on Ricardian equivalence, concludes that such effects halve the impact of policy. This is consistent with our results, as it is the lack of a Ricardian offset which makes idiosyncratic federal deficits more effective.
19 See Frenkel *et al.* (1991) and Bayoumi and Sterne (1993). The results quoted subsequently in the text are derived from Bayoumi and Sterne.
20 Japan, South Korea, Taiwan, Hong Kong, Singapore, Australia, New Zealand, Indonesia, Thailand, Malaysia, and the Philippines.
21 Mussa *et al.* (1994).
22 However, the Commission of the European Community (1990) notes that most of the increase in trade in Europe has been within industries. Accordingly, they argue that increased specialization will have little effect on the desirability of a common currency.
23 For example Stockman (1988) and Norrbin and Schlagenhauf (1988, 1994). A high proportion of industry-specific disturbances was interpreted as evidence for real business cycle theories, and region-specific disturbances as evidence against them. Bayoumi and Prasad (1995) review this literature.
24 Borio (1996).
25 Alesina and Summers (1993).
26 On the other hand, the information age may well lower the costs of transactions between currencies, and thus the benefits of a single currency. I, for one, now regularly use my bank card to get money in Europe from automatic teller machines, thereby reducing the costs and hassle of changing money at banks or other financial institutions.
27 See International Monetary Fund (1984) for a survey and Gagnon (1993) for a discussion of more recent results. Frankel and Wei (1993), using a particularly large data set involving bilateral trade between 63 countries, found that while exchange rate volatility had a statistically significant impact on trade, that effect was small. For example, a doubling of the level of real exchange rate volatility in Europe in 1990 (which would have returned such variability to its 1980, pre-ERM, level) would have lowered intra-regional trade volumes by only 0.7 percent.
28 Goldberg (1993).

29 Mussa *et al.* (1994).

30 However, much of this boost to trade could come through provisions for greater integration of goods and capital markets, of the type envisaged by the Single Market program in the EU, rather than from a single currency.

31 One example is a study of the losses to the US economy in 1890 if the railroad had not been invented (Fogel, 1964), by that time the dominant form of transportation. Assuming perfect competition, the loss was a mere 6 percent of gross national product, as the resources used in the railroads could be reallocated to other, only marginally less efficient, uses.

32 Masson and Symansky (1992) provide a useful overview of many of the technical issues involved, in addition to reporting their own results and reviewing earlier work. See also Commission of the European Communities (1990).

33 Most of the existing literature on the choice of exchange rate regime, which is focused on developing countries, uses only a limited number of optimum currency area variables (Savvides, 1993, gives a survey). Some results on the relationship between exchange rate volatility and optimum currency area variables for industrial countries are contained in Bayoumi and Eichengreen (1997).

7 Economic integration and optimum currency areas

The existing analysis of optimum currency areas generally takes a static approach to the issue, asking whether a set of regions is currently in a position to form a currency union.[1] In practice, however, there is an important dynamic element to the choice of a single currency, as the adoption of a single money is generally associated with a move toward greater economic (and political) integration. This is most obvious in the case of western Europe, where proposals for a single currency are explicitly linked to the need to generate greater integration of the regional economy.[2]

While it is clear that a single currency promotes economic integration, it is much less clear that economic integration increases the attractiveness of a single currency. Two opposing views have been put forward in the literature. Krugman (1993) argues that greater integration is likely to make Europe a less good candidate for a single currency. He notes the greater regional concentration of industries in the United States compared with Europe, and suggests that this reflects the existence of a single currency. A single currency in Europe would, he argues, make the European economy more regionally concentrated. This would make the economy more susceptible to asymmetric regional shocks, as industry-specific disturbances will have a larger regional impact. For example, if all European cars were made in Germany (in the same way that all automobiles in the United States are made in the midwest), then a downturn in demand would translate into a negative economic shock to Germany but not to the rest of the Union. Hence, economic integration makes disturbances to the car industry into German-specific shocks.

On the other hand, the Commission of the European Communities (1990) argues that increased integration will improve the operation of

118

a single currency. This is because the specialization will occur within industries, and hence the impact of an industry-wide shock will be more diffuse, and because a single currency will eliminate the economic disruption between countries caused by unexpected exchange rate changes. In this view, a single currency generates a virtuous circle in which the greater integration makes it easier to operate a currency union.

This chapter provides a framework for analyzing the connection between a single currency, economic integration, and regional disturbances. This allows the alternative hypotheses outlined above to be examined and compared in a formal manner, thereby providing a method for assessing the merits of each approach. At the same time, the limitations of such an exercise should be borne in mind. The analysis focuses on the relationship between underlying disturbances and economic integration, to the exclusion of other potential dynamic factors. In particular, the formal model does not encompass the possibility that greater integration could improve adjustment to regional disturbances through other channels, for example by increasing labor market flexibility as labor markets become more integrated, or by reducing the political barriers to regional fiscal transfers. These factors are, however, discussed in a less formal manner within the context of the model.

The next section of the chapter outlines a simple model of trade between industries in a regional economy, and looks at the consequences of greater economic integration for the underlying disturbances faced by the regions. The section after extends this model to a two-industry model of the aggregate economy, and discusses the role of the exchange rate in restoring equilibrium. This is followed by a more general discussion of the connection between optimum currency areas and integration, and some conclusions.

The model

Consider an economy with two regions, X and M. In each region industry i is assumed to produce goods which are perfect substitutes. Both industries are assumed to be competitive and to face decreasing returns to scale, so that there is a conventional upward-sloping supply curve in each region. However, underlying costs differ across the two locations, due to differing natural advantages, so that the marginal product schedules and hence the supply curves in each region are distinct. For simplicity, the underlying demand curves for the good are assumed to be identical in each region.

The process of integration is modeled by including a fixed cost, ϕ, per good for moving products from one region to another. This cost covers changing money and complying with different legal codes, as well as simple transportation. It allows the price of the good to differ between the two regions by reducing the incentive to trade. Greater integration can then be modeled as a reduction in the cost of trading goods, ϕ. Such a reduction in costs increases output in the more efficient region, decreases it in the less efficient region, and increases the level of trade.

This can be shown by solving the model. Assume that the supply curves for the regions are given by:

$$S_i = A_i + B_i P \tag{7.1}$$

where A_i and B_i are fixed parameters, and P is the price received by the producer net of transport costs. The assumption that production is more efficient in region X than in region M can be imposed by assuming that $A_X > A_M$ and $B_X > B_M$, where subscript X refers to the exporting region and subscript M to the importing region. Demand, which is assumed identical in each region, is given by:

$$D_i = C - D P \tag{7.2}$$

where C and D are again fixed parameters. The assumption that the demand curves are identical has no material effect on the analysis, but it simplifies some of the calculations and ensures that region X, which produces more of the good, exports to region M.

Equilibrium requires that aggregate supply and aggregate demand for the good is equal across the two regions. Assuming that the differential in efficiency is large enough to dominate the costs of transportation, and hence that goods are exported from region X to region M, it also requires that the price of the good in region M is ϕ greater that the price in region X. This is the only point at which the producer price (i.e., the selling price of the good net of transport costs) is the same in both regions for producers in region X, which sell goods in both markets. Equilibrium is thus defined as:

$$S_X(P_X) + S_M(P_M) = D_X(P_X) + D_M(P_M) \qquad (7.3)$$

$$P_M = P_X + \phi \qquad (7.4)$$

Trade from region X to region M (labeled T) is then equal to the difference between demand and supply in regions:

$$T = D_M - S_M = S_X - D_X \qquad (7.5)$$

Using the assumed functional forms, this produces the following results:

$$P_X = \eta - \kappa\phi$$
$$P_M = \eta + (1-\kappa)\phi$$
$$Y_X = A_X + B_X(\eta-\kappa\phi) \qquad (7.6)$$
$$Y_M = A_M + B_M(\eta+(1-\kappa)\phi)$$
$$T = (C-A_M) - (B_M+D)(\eta+(1-\kappa)\phi)$$

where Y_X and Y_M are outputs of the good in regions X and M respectively, and η and κ are constants such that:

$$\eta = (2C-A_X-A_M)/(B_X+B_M+2D)$$

and $$\kappa = (B_X+D)/(B_X+B_M+2D)$$

Note that κ is necessarily between 0 and 1. The equilibrium is illustrated in Figure 7.1, which shows supply and demand in the two regions.

Lowering transaction costs increases output and prices in region X, decreases them in region M, and increases the level of trade. In short, it produces an increase in specialization in production towards the more efficient region, which, in turn, produces a greater level of trade. These results are largely independent of many of the specific assumptions made in this derivation. For example, the demand curve does not have to be identical in the two regions, or even to have the same slope. All that is required for these basic results is that the costs of transaction are low enough for producers in region X to find it profitable to export their goods to region M.

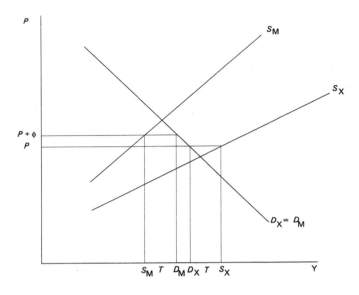

Figure 7.1 The trade model

The next stage is to expand the analysis to consider the impact of disturbances to supply or demand. This is done by including disturbances in each of the equations. Hence, for example, the supply curve in region X becomes:

$$S_X = A_X + B_X P + B_X \varepsilon_X^s \qquad (7.7)$$

where ε_X^s is a period-specific disturbance to the supply function. Similar disturbances are added to the supply curve in region M and to the two demand curves. The dependence of supply shocks in region X on the parameter B_X reflects the fact that shocks which lower costs by equal amounts will have bigger effects on output in the region which produces more of the good. The disturbance to supply in region M, ε_M^s, is similarly multiplied by the slope of the supply curve, B_M. The two demand shocks are also assumed to depend upon the slope of the demand curves, D.

Maintaining the assumption that, even in the face of these underlying disturbances, the underlying pattern of trade – that region X exports to region M – remains unchanged, the resulting equilibrium is:

$$P_X = \eta - \kappa\phi + \frac{D\varepsilon_X^D + D\varepsilon_M^D - B_X\varepsilon_X^S - B_M\varepsilon_M^S}{B_X + B_M + 2D}$$

$$P_M = \eta + (1 - \kappa)\phi + \frac{D\varepsilon_X^D + D\varepsilon_M^D - B_X\varepsilon_X^S - B_M\varepsilon_M^S}{B_X + B_M + 2D}$$

$$Y_X = A_X + B_X(\eta - \kappa\phi) + B_X\frac{D\varepsilon_X^D + D\varepsilon_M^D + (B_M + 2D)\varepsilon_X^S - B_M\varepsilon_M^S}{B_X + B_M + 2D}$$

$$\text{(7.8)}$$

$$Y_M = A_M + B_M(\eta + (1 - \kappa)\phi) + B_M\frac{D\varepsilon_X^D + D\varepsilon_M^D - B_X\varepsilon_X^S + (B_X + 2D)\varepsilon_M^S}{B_X + B_M + 2D}$$

$$T = (C - A_M) - (B_M + D)(\eta + (1 - \kappa)\phi)$$
$$+ \frac{-D(B_M + D)\varepsilon_X^D + (B_X + D)D\varepsilon_M^D + (B_X(B_M + 2D) - DB_M)\varepsilon_X^S - (B_X + D)B_M\varepsilon_M^S}{B_X + B_M + 2D}$$

$$Y_X - Y_M = (A_X - A_M) + (B_X - B_M)\eta - \frac{(B_X + B_M + D)(B_X - B_M)}{B_X + B_M + 2D}\phi$$
$$+ \frac{(B_X - B_M)D((\varepsilon_X^D + \varepsilon_M^D) - (\varepsilon_X^S + \varepsilon_M^S)) + (2B_XB_M + D(B_X + B_M))(\varepsilon_X^S - \varepsilon_M^S)}{B_X + B_M + 2D}$$

As can be seen from the final terms in the price equations (P_X and P_M), all the demand and supply disturbances have the same effect on price levels in both regions. This is because trade flows are sufficiently flexible to maintain regional arbitrage in goods prices, with the cost of transportation ensuring that the price in the importing region is ϕ higher than that in the exporting region. As demand disturbances affect supply and output only through their effect on prices, *the location of the shocks to demand has no impact on the allocation of final output between the two regions.* Positive demand shocks, whatever their location, raise prices and output in both locations. Demand shocks do, however, generate asymmetric output responses across the two regions, reflecting the divergence in slopes of the underlying supply curves, and hence the different marginal rates of supply of output created by a change in prices. This can be seen from the term in the sum of demand shocks ($\varepsilon_X^D + \varepsilon_M^D$) in the equation for the differences in output across the two regions ($Y_X - Y_M$). The irrelevance of the location of the demand shocks to the final outcome is reflected in the absence of a term in the difference between the two demand shocks in this equation.

Supply shocks have a more complex impact on output. A positive supply shock in either location raises output in that region. It also

lowers output in the other region, as increased supply lowers prices
and hence the incentive to produce. Thus, while demand shocks have
an effect which is generally similar across regions – a demand shock
moves output in both regions in the same direction – supply shocks
have a dissimilar effect across regions. This can be seen in the term in
the difference between the two supply shocks ($\varepsilon_X^S - \varepsilon_M^S$) in the equation
for relative output across the two regions. As in the case of demand
shocks, differences in the slopes of the supply curves across the two
regions also mean that symmetric supply shocks, in which the industry
experiences the same sized underlying disturbance in both regions,
also have asymmetric effects on output. This can be seen from the
($\varepsilon_X^S + \varepsilon_M^S$) term in the formula for the differences in output responses
across the two regions ($Y_X - Y_M$). However, a comparison of the
coefficients indicate that asymmetric supply disturbances ($\varepsilon_X^S - \varepsilon_M^S$)
have a much larger impact on relative output than do symmetric
disturbances ($\varepsilon_X^S + \varepsilon_M^S$). Finally, note that the impact of both demand
and supply shocks on net exports (T) depends upon their location,
with negative local demand shocks and positive local supply shocks
improving the trade balance for the region concerned, while for the
other two shocks the impact is the opposite.

In short, two considerations define the size of the asymmetric
shocks to output. The first is the 'compositional' effect caused by
differences in the slopes of underlying supply functions across regions. This applies to all demand shocks and to symmetric supply
shocks. The second is the more powerful direct effects on output
caused by asymmetric supply shocks.

This division of the types of disturbance corresponds to that used in
empirical work looking at the sources of shocks across industries and
regions, such as Bini-Smaghi and Vori (1993), Bayoumi and Prasad
(1995), and Ghosh and Wolf (1996), which try to identify whether
shocks are industry or region specific. As there is only one industry in
the analysis above, symmetric disturbances in the model can be thought
of as being industry-specific disturbances, while asymmetric disturbances are region-specific. Equations (7.8) indicate that even
symmetric disturbances can have an impact on relative output because
of differences in the supply response. This implies that account needs
to be taken of the structure of output across regions when estimating
the net impact of different types of underlying disturbance. In particular, industry-specific shocks, which are generally identified in the
empirical literature as those shocks which have the same percentage

impact on output across industries in different regions (or countries), will have significant asymmetric effects on aggregate output when there are large differences in the relative size of the industry across regions.[3] On this basis, the less industrially diversified Europe might be considered a better candidate for a currency union than the more specialized United States even if the size of the underlying shocks was similar.

Results for the full economy and the role of the exchange rate

This section expands the results from a single industry to the economy as a whole, and explores the role of the exchange rate within such a model. The whole economy is represented by considering two industries, one of which exports products from one region to the other, while the other industry exports products in the other direction. The two industries are assumed to be identical in other respects. In particular, the underlying parameters in the supply functions for both exporting regional industries and both importing regional industries are assumed to be the same. As in the earlier analysis, the demand functions are assumed to be identical across regions and industries. Finally, capital markets are assumed to be open, so that consumers and producers are able to borrow and lend freely across regions. As a result, demand in any particular region is not constrained by the behavior of local supply, and hence disturbances to the underlying functions can be analyzed independently from each other.[4] More restricted capital markets imply more complex interactions in the response to underlying demand and supply disturbances, as will be discussed further below.

These assumptions about the economy are clearly restrictive. Limiting the whole economy to only two industries increases the importance of idiosyncratic shocks to the economy as a whole. However, the equilibrium for an economy with many industries, some net exporters and some net importers, can be easily derived from the simpler case which has only two industries. The two-industry case can therefore be seen as a simplified version which helps to illustrate the features of a fuller and richer, but by the same token more complex, multi-industry model. The two-industry model also fails to deal with the argument of the Commission of the European Communities that specialization will occur within industries, not between them. This implies that integration will make supply curves across regions within an industry more similar. The impact of such a change will also be discussed below. Finally, the model takes no account of supply and demand from outside the two regions.

In what follows, the X and M subscripts are used to define the underlying coefficients for the exporting and importing industries, the two regions are subscripted by α and β, and the two industries by 1 and 2. For simplicity, only deviations from underlying levels of output are reported. As the results for each individual industry are the same as the results for a single industry reported earlier, we will limit ourselves to considering aggregate output across the two industries within the regions. Adding the output of the two industries together to get output for each region as a whole gives the following results:

$$
Y_\alpha = \frac{B_X D(\varepsilon_{1a}^D + \varepsilon_{1\beta}^D) + B_M D(\varepsilon_{2a}^D + \varepsilon_{2\beta}^D)}{B_X + B_M + 2D}
$$
$$
+ \frac{B_X B_M(\varepsilon_{1a}^S + \varepsilon_{2a}^S - \varepsilon_{1\beta}^S - \varepsilon_{2\beta}^S) + 2DB_X\varepsilon_{1a}^S + 2DB_M\varepsilon_{2a}^S}{B_X + B_M + 2D}
$$

$$
Y_\beta = \frac{B_X D(\varepsilon_{2a}^D + \varepsilon_{2\beta}^D) + B_M D(\varepsilon_{1a}^D + \varepsilon_{1\beta}^D)}{B_X + B_M + 2D}
$$
$$
+ \frac{B_X B_M(\varepsilon_{1\beta}^S + \varepsilon_{2\beta}^S - \varepsilon_{1a}^S - \varepsilon_{2a}^S) + 2DB_X\varepsilon_{2\beta}^S + 2DB_M\varepsilon_{1\beta}^S}{B_X + B_M + 2D}
$$

(7.9)

$$
Y_\alpha - Y_\beta = \frac{2(B_X - B_M)D(\varepsilon_{1a}^D + \varepsilon_{1\beta}^D - \varepsilon_{2a}^D - \varepsilon_{2\beta}^D)}{B_X + B_M + 2D}
$$
$$
+ \frac{(D(B_X + B_M) + 2B_X B_M)(\varepsilon_{1a}^S - \varepsilon_{1\beta}^S + \varepsilon_{2a}^S - \varepsilon_{2\beta}^S)}{B_X + B_M + 2D}
$$
$$
+ \frac{D(B_X - B_M)(\varepsilon_{1a}^S + \varepsilon_{1\beta}^S - \varepsilon_{2a}^S - \varepsilon_{2\beta}^S)}{B_X + B_M + 2D}
$$

These equations illustrate many of the themes found in the model for a single industry. In particular, demand shocks affect relative output between the two regions only through the effect of aggregate demand for each good on relative supply across the two regions. The regional location of disturbances to demand for each good is not important. In addition, as the effect on relative output of a rise in demand for the goods of the exporting industry is the precise opposite of the impact on relative output from the same stimulus in the importing industry, demand shocks that are equal across the industries have no net impact on relative output.

Supply shocks affect relative output largely, although not exclusively, through differences in the location of supply shocks across regions. The effect is captured in the first of the two terms for supply shocks in the equation for changes in relative output $(Y_\alpha - Y_\beta)$. This term, $(\varepsilon^S_{1\alpha} - \varepsilon^S_{1\beta} + \varepsilon^S_{2\alpha} - \varepsilon^S_{2\beta})$, which shows the impact of relative supply shocks between the two regions, operates largely through the direct impact on supply in the region concerned. The second term in supply shocks, $(\varepsilon^S_{1\alpha} + \varepsilon^S_{1\beta} - \varepsilon^S_{2\alpha} - \varepsilon^S_{2\beta})$, shows the impact of supply shocks which are different across industries, but not across regions. Such industry-specific supply disturbances cause output across regions to diverge for similar reasons to that for demand shocks (i.e., through differences in the supply response to a given change in prices). A comparison of the coefficients on the two types of disturbance indicates that these industry-specific supply disturbances clearly have a secondary effect on output compared with the region-specific ones discussed earlier. In short, the two types of disturbance – region specific and industry specific – generally operate on relative output between the two regions in rather different ways.

Expanding the analysis to the whole economy allows the exchange rate to be incorporated into the model. Before considering the potential impact of the exchange rate on the equilibrium, however, it is necessary to discuss the meaning of the underlying supply functions that have been used to date. If these curves trace the optimum allocation of resources in a fully flexible economy, then the exchange rate has no real role in the analysis. This is simply an alternative way of looking at the fact that the choice of exchange rate regime is essentially irrelevant in a world with fully flexible prices.

If, however, the supply curves are assumed to represent responses generated by nominal rigidities of some kind, so that movements away from the underlying equilibrium on the supply curve reflect disruptive changes in the economy, the exchange rate can help to move the economy back closer to its underlying equilibrium. The exchange rate cannot fully eliminate these disequilibria, in part because the area as a whole may be subject to aggregate disturbances. If both regions are hit by shocks that leave their economies either above or below capacity in aggregate, then the exchange rate can determine only the relative degree to which the two regions are affected. In addition, unless factors of production are perfectly mobile across different industries within a region, then industries within a region will face different conditions. For example, while (say) footwear is doing well in a region and tending to operate above potential, computer manufacturers may be in the doldrums. As the exchange rate uniformly changes relative prices in one region compared with other regions, reducing the disequilibrium in one industry in this situation may well tend to exacerbate it in the other. This does not mean that the exchange rate is not useful in reducing economy-wide disequilibria, even in such circumstances. If footwear is a relatively minor industry in a region while computers are very important, for example, then a depreciation in the exchange rate which boosts output in both industries may well move the economy as a whole back toward equilibrium, even as it increases the degree to which the footwear industry operates above potential.

The impact of a change in the exchange rate can be modeled as an equi-proportional change in prices in region α compared with region β. Using the linear approximation that prices of both goods in region α rise by a constant amount, e, compared with those in region β – which is equivalent in this model to an appreciation in the currency of region α compared with β – reduces output of industry 1 and industry 2 in region α by $(B_X(B_M+D)/(B_X+B_M+2D))e$ and $(B_M(B_X+D)/(B_X+B_M+2D))e$, respectively. Output of these same industries in region β rise by $(B_M(B_M+D)/(B_X+B_M+2D))e$ and $(B_X(B_X+D)/(B_X+B_M+2D))e$. Hence, exchange rate changes can be used partially to offset the impact of unexpected demand and supply shocks upon the economy. The response is most effective in the face of economy-wide supply shocks which reduce output in all industries within a region compared with its neighbors. It is less effective, but can still have some result, when the underlying shocks are industry-specific.

Finally, the impact of changes in the value of the exchange rate on output is a useful way of approaching the issue of how lower levels of capital mobility between the two regions might change the results. If capital mobility is low, the trade balance will be small, so the exchange rate will tend to move so as to reduce the aggregate trade balance between the two regions. The implications of lower capital mobility can therefore be explored by considering the exchange rate response required to move the trade balance back to its original value in response to the various types of shock. The discussion will be on an intuitive level, as the mathematical results are complex and add little to the analysis. As can be seen from the results for a single industry, positive demand shocks in the importing region or positive supply shocks in the exporting region tend to increase the exporters' trade balance, while positive demand shocks in the exporting region or supply shocks in the importing region lowers it. Low capital mobility will tend to generate exchange rate movements which will offset these changes in the trade balance, so that the exchange rate of the exporter will tend to appreciate in the face of positive foreign demand shocks or local supply shocks and fall in the face of local demand or foreign supply shocks. This exchange rate response will reduce the impact of a disturbance on movements in relative output in most cases (this is not the case, however, for demand shocks in the exporting region). Lower capital mobility may thus tend to reduce relative output fluctuations across regions.

Integration and optimum currency areas

This theoretical apparatus can now be used to examine the impact of increased economic integration upon the economy. The most striking feature of the analysis is the absence of the integration parameter, ϕ, in the equations defining the responses of the economy to demand and supply shocks. Hence, in this very simple demand and supply model, *the effect of the demand and supply shocks on output is independent of the level of integration of the economies.* While changes in the cost of transportation change underlying levels of output and net exports across industries, these changes have no impact on the way in which these various types of shock move the economies away from these underlying values.

This result does not necessarily mean that increasing integration has no impact on the response of the economy to disturbances, and hence its suitability for a single currency. What is does imply, however, is that such changes must come through modifications to the structure of the basic demand and supply model. Several such modifications spring to mind. Greater trade integration can be expected to make the economies more specialized in production, thereby altering the slopes of the underlying supply curves. More radically, greater integration could change the nature of regional trading relationships. For example, the reduction in costs of transportation could make it economic to initiate trade in goods which were originally supplied solely by domestic sources. It could also lead to complete regional specialization of production, in which industries agglomerate in a single region rather than operating in both regions simultaneously.[5] Finally, trade (and capital market) integration could change the nature of the underlying disturbances to demand and supply.

Let us first consider the impact of changes in the slopes of the underlying supply and demand curves. As shown earlier for a single industry, lower transportation costs increase the level of specialization of production and trade across regions. The obvious corollary of such a shift in production is an increase in the response of supply to price changes in the industries which are net exporters of goods, and a reduction in the response of industries which are net importers. In terms of the model discussed above, the coefficient B_X can be expected to increase, while B_M will tend to fall. This will tend to increase the differential impact of demand and of industry-specific supply shocks on output in the two regions, as can be seen from the formula for relative output movements in equations (7.9). The reason is that shocks which affect a single industry in a uniform manner will produce more diversity in output responses across the two regions as production becomes more specialized. Assuming that the rise in the B_X coefficient is equal to the reduction in the B_M coefficient, however, there will be a small fall in the impact of region-specific supply shocks on differential output across the two regions, because the spill-over effect of foreign supply shocks on domestic output declines.[6]

Overall, these changes will tend to decrease the attraction of a common currency area across regions in which demand or industry-specific supply disturbances are relatively important, and which are well suited for a currency union. However, it may slightly increase the attraction of a common currency for regions where regional supply disturbances are more prevalent, and which are therefore less well suited to a currency union. This case illustrates the concerns of Krugman (1993) that integration will tend to decrease the attractiveness of a common currency.

Greater integration could also increase competition across firms, thereby making supply in both regions more responsive to change in price. In terms of the framework, this can be seen as a rise in both B_X and B_M. Assuming that both coefficients rise by equal amounts, so that B_X-B_M remains unchanged, equations (7.9) imply that the coefficients on demand disturbances and on industry-specific supply disturbances in the equation for relative output $(Y_\alpha - Y_\beta)$ will fall, while those on region-specific disturbances will rise.[7] Hence, this case is the mirror image of the example just analyzed. Now integration will tend to increase the attraction of a common currency area across regions where demand or industry-specific supply disturbances are prevalent, while potentially decreasing the attraction of a common currency for regions with more regional supply disturbances. This case corresponds to that discussed by the Commission of the European Communities (1990), which notes that increased competition will make a currency union easier to operate as producers will have more incentive to cushion price shocks through changes in margins.

The framework is also capable of looking at the consequences of shifts in the nature of trade between the two regions. Integration could cause a shift from no trading at all to one in which goods are exchanged across regions. If there is initially no trade, there is also no role for the exchange rate in reducing economic disturbances across regions. Greater integration, by stimulating trade, provides the exchange rate with such a role. The implications for the advisability of a currency union depends upon the role of the industry within the domestic cycle. For highly cyclical industries, the effect will be positive, as trade can help reduce the effects of the business cycle. For industries which tend to dampen the cycle, on the other hand, the opening of trade with other regions may well reduce this stabilizing role.

Integration could also lead to the complete specialization of production in one region, reflecting, for example, the existence of increasing returns to scale due to fixed costs, as emphasized in 'new theories of international trade'[8] and recent work on the 'new economic geography.'[9] The results from this change are simply a more extreme version of the changes caused by the opposite movements in B_X and B_M analyzed earlier. Industry-specific disturbances become more disruptive – indeed, in the case of completely specialized production, industry-specific disturbances are essentially equivalent to region-specific disturbances because of the single location of production. At the same time, there is a slight decline in the overall impact on relative output from supply disturbances which affect all industries within a region equally, as the spill-over effects from foreign supply disturbances become smaller.

In addition to changing supply curves for products, integration could also change the nature of the underlying disturbances faced across regions. One potential source of such disturbances is the exchange rate itself. Empirically, movements of floating exchange rates appear to be highly unpredictable, as would be anticipated from theories which view the exchange rate as an asset price.[10] If exchange rates also exhibit 'excess volatility,' so that their movements are largely unrelated to fundamentals, then the exchange rate itself can become the source of disruptive disturbances across regions. The role of the exchange rate in influencing relative output across regions has not been thoroughly researched, although some results from a framework that assumes that exchange rates cushion the impact of output fluctuations are presented in Bayoumi and Thomas (1995). Hence, it remains unclear whether the removal of the exchange rate will increase the disruption to relative output as one form of adjustment is lost, as assumed in much of the theory of optimum currency areas, or reduce disruption to relative output as excess volatility in exchange rates is reduced.

Greater integration could also change the nature of demand and supply disturbances across regions. One such avenue is through greater financial integration. Limited capital mobility can be seen as a constraint on the degree of independence between demand and supply shocks, either directly or through the exchange rate response required to limit net trade imbalances across regions. As discussed earlier, low capital mobility will generally dampen shocks to relative output overall.

There are several other avenues through which greater integration could affect underlying disturbances. For example, it could generate more coordination of government policies at both the macroeconomic and microeconomic levels. As such policies are one component in creating demand and supply disturbances for individual industries, this could generate greater coherence in disturbances across regions. A common currency could also make labor markets more flexible. Such changes would be expected to make a currency union easier to create. Finally, greater competition in product markets could also change the nature of underlying disturbances, although in this case the direction of change is less clear. On the one hand, greater incentives for innovation could mean that disturbances are larger. On the other hand, market discipline may limit the impact of such changes on output.

Conclusions

This chapter has provided a framework within which to consider how greater integration of trade, caused by lowering the costs of exporting goods between regions, might affect the suitability of such regions to become a currency union. One reason for providing such a framework is that earlier discussions of this issue have come to very different conclusions, with some emphasizing the potential for idiosyncratic disturbances across regions to become larger as regions become more specialized in production, while others have noted the potential for exchange rates themselves to be a disruptive force, causing output across differing currency unions to diverge.

The results from this chapter provide some support for both sides of the debate, in that the model can be used to demonstrate the potential impact of both these types of factor on relative output across regions. However, the most important result from this chapter is probably a relatively negative one, namely that trade integration need not, in and of itself, lead to any changes in responses to underlying disturbances. The impact of greater integration of trade may therefore be a second-ary factor on optimum currency area analysis. This result is consistent with earlier empirical work. For example, Bayoumi and Eichengreen (1993a) identified no clear changes in the nature of the underlying aggregate demand and supply disturbances coming from the increas-ing integration in Europe since the 1960s created by the development of the EC, or, as it has been recently renamed, the EU.

This does not mean that greater integration is irrelevant for success-ful currency unions. Clearly, close economic integration between regions is a key characteristic of areas with single currencies. What it does imply, however, is that the level of this integration may not be a key issue when determining the suitability of an area for a single currency, at least in terms of movements in relative output. Such a conclusion has the significant advantage of implying that comparisons of movements of relative output between regions with very different levels of integration, such as states within the United States and countries within the EU, are probably quite useful guides as to their relative suitability for a currency union.

Finally, the simplicity of the theoretical framework outlined in this chapter should be emphasized. Numerous extensions and adaptations could be imagined. To take just two examples, no account was taken in the analysis of product differentiation across goods, as used in 'new' theories of international trade, or of trade from economies outside the two regions. These, and other, issues remain to be explored.

Notes

1 This work was surveyed in the previous two chapters.

2 Similarly, in cases where currency unions have been abandoned, this has been accompanied by a significant reduction in economic integration. Recent examples of this process include the break-up of the rouble zone among the countries of the former Soviet Union, and the split of the former Czechoslovakia into the Czech Republic and Slovakia (see Commission of the European Communities, 1990).

3 Hence the focus on industrial structure as a characteristic of an optimum currency area (Kenen, 1969). This characteristic can help to explain why disturbances appear to become more industry specific as the number of industries which are identified in the analysis increases (Ghosh and Wolf, 1996). As industries become more finely differentiated, they also become more regionally concentrated, blurring the difference between industry-specific and region-specific disturbances.

4 In a fully articulated intertemporal system, movements in net asset holdings between the two countries will cause trends in relative income and demand. We abstract from such longer-term considerations so as to focus on responses to short-term disturbances.

5 As emphasized in the literature on the 'new economic geography,' for example Krugman (1991b) and Krugman and Venables (1996). See Fujita and Thisse (1996) for a survey.

6 Specifically, the $B_X B_M$ term in the numerator will fall.

7 This analysis assumes that there is no reduction in the size of the underlying supply disturbances. In the model these disturbances are measured in terms of their impact on prices (recall that in the supply equation the disturbances are multiplied by B_X or B_M). If the size of the disturbances are reduced proportionately to the rise in the underlying parameters, the results would tend to indicate an even stronger conclusion, namely that greater competition would reduce the impact of all supply and demand shocks on relative output, making a currency union more attractive in all circumstances.

8 Krugman (1980) and Helpman and Krugman (1986).

9 Krugman and Venables (1996).

10 Meese and Rogoff (1983).

8 Concluding observations

This book has critically reviewed the academic literature on two areas of international finance: capital mobility and optimum currency areas. The theme which links these topics is the interaction between the integration of financial markets and the real economy. In discussing capital mobility, the focus has been on exploring how the financial regime affects real behavior. Accordingly, the text largely concentrated on tests of capital mobility using measures of real activity, exploring how financial integration affects both correlations between saving and investment and patterns of consumption. Reversing the causation, the theory of optimum currency areas explores the impact of real behavior on the choice of the monetary regime. It therefore explores how the behavior of the real economy can affect financial integration.[1]

Reviewing both sides of the interaction between financial integration and the real economy allows a less partial, more holistic, view of the relationship between the financial regime and real activity. Gaining an understanding of this relationship is particularly relevant at the current moment, given the speedy recent opening of international capital markets[2] and the prospect of a single European currency before the end of the decade.

International financial integration

The dominant theme in most recent work on capital mobility has been explaining the apparent dichotomy between 'market' tests of capital mobility and tests using 'real' variables. More explicitly, tests using market prices, such as comparisons of onshore–offshore interest rates, find capital mobility to be currently very high, as might be expected given recent moves toward dismantling controls on international capital movements. By contrast, tests which look at the implications of high capital mobility for real decisions, such as saving, investment, and consumption, tend to find that the observed behavior across countries is not consistent with high capital mobility.

The standard explanation for the dichotomy between these tests of capital mobility is to assume that the 'market' tests are correct while the tests of capital mobility based on 'real' variables are misspecified. It is argued that, while the observed behavior of saving, investment, and consumption across countries may appear to be inconsistent with high capital mobility, this reflects the simplicity of the underlying theories from which the tests are derived. The apparent inconsistencies between capital mobility and real behavior across countries can be reconciled when more complex theoretical considerations are taken into account. Much recent work on capital mobility has thus been focused on presenting theoretical models in which capital mobility is high and these stylized facts – high correlations of saving and investment rates, and a close correspondence between movements in disposable income and consumption across countries – are observed. The implication is that capital mobility is indeed high across (industrial) countries.

A weakness with this line of reasoning is that demonstrating that observed behavior *can* be consistent with the assumption of high capital mobility is not the same as showing that capital mobility is indeed high. An alternative approach to deciding whether the simple tests of capital mobility using real variables are adequate is to examine the results from these tests in environments where capital mobility is known to be high, such as between regions within a country. Results from these natural experiments indicate that the behavior within countries corresponds quite closely to that predicted by the simple tests. These results tend to undermine the view that the tests using real variables are misspecified.

If misspecification does not explain the divergence in results between the two types of test of capital mobility, what does? My answer is that 'market' tests of capital mobility and tests involving 'real' variables look at different concepts, and hence there is nothing necessarily inconsistent about having different results from the two approaches. 'Market' tests measure *access* to international capital markets. If it is relatively simple and cheap to transfer (say) US dollar deposits between the United States and the rest of the world, then one would expect onshore–offshore interest rate differentials to be small, owing to arbitrage. This is indeed what occurs, indicating that access to capital markets is currently high. Hence, on this basis international capital is indeed highly mobile.

Tests using real variables, whether based on correlations of saving and investment or on consumption patterns, look at a different aspect of capital mobility, namely whether individuals are *using* international capital markets to improve the intertemporal allocation of resources. Intertemporal trades require that international capital markets not only are open now, but that they are expected to remain open in the future, or, in some cases, that they were open in the past (when the original transaction would have had to have been made). Individuals not only have to have access to international capital markets, in other words, they also have to use them. Hence, capital mobility tests of whether capital markets are open using real variables, namely whether individuals are actually using capital markets to improve their livelihood, are more stringent than 'market' tests.[3] They test the benefits of capital mobility, not access to markets.

From this perspective, the divergent results from the two types of test of capital mobility do not necessarily involve any inconsistency. It is perfectly possible that individuals have access to international capital markets currently but are not fully using them for intertemporal trades, if uncertainties remain over access to these markets in the future. To take an extreme case, consider a world in which capital markets were open today, but it is known with certainty that they will be shut down tomorrow for ever. Clearly, not much intertemporal trade would occur even though access to capital markets was high.

Concerns about the ability to use capital markets in the future are likely to be much more important across currency unions than within them. It is very unusual to try to limit capital flows within a currency union, in part because money is so fungible. Changing currencies, however, provides a convenient point at which to impose government regulation. Hence, while the world has certainly gone through long periods of open capital markets between countries (the classical gold standard period springs to mind), the very existence of separate currencies provides the potential for future controls on capital movements. Because of this possibility, separate currencies may tend to limit intertemporal trades even if international capital markets are currently open.

Optimum currency areas

Unlike capital mobility, the literature on optimum currency areas (OCA) has no outstanding academic controversy to give it forward momentum. After a burst of activity in the 1960s and early 1970s, interest in OCA theory rapidly waned.

The recent revival of interest in this topic stems from a specific policy initiative, namely plans for EMU. As these plans have become ever more concrete and well defined, there has been a steady increase in interest in OCA theory. Indeed, most of the debate about the economic desirability of EMU has been couched in OCA terms, as the theory provides a coherent basis for discussing the merits of introducing a common currency. This is true in spite of the fact that many commentators have remained somewhat skeptical as to the practical value of the theory. Such skepticism stems from several sources. One is the relatively unstructured nature of the underlying theoretical ideas. The theory was developed by several academics in the 1960s with rather different focuses, and its underpinnings have remained somewhat diffuse. A second concern is the lack of strong tests of the theory. Monetary unions are only rarely altered, and information on behavior within currency unions, which is important in terms of testing the implications of the theory, is relatively limited.[4]

The discussion on optimum currency areas in this book addressed some of these concerns. It started with a review of the underlying theory which put an emphasis on integrating various contributions into a single structure. This was followed by a critical review of the empirical evidence, focusing on the extent to which the ideas behind the theory have been successfully implemented, and on whether the factors identified by OCA theory matter for existing currency unions. The emphasis throughout was on the implications of recent empirical work, largely focused on Europe, for OCA theory – as opposed to the more usual question of what work on OCA theory implies for EMU. The conclusions are fairly positive. Considerable progress has been made in operationalizing the underlying theoretical concepts. Furthermore, these factors do appear to matter for actual currency unions.

One difficulty with the current state of work on OCA theory is that it is largely static. Most work simply tests whether a region is part of an OCA or not. In practice, however, important dynamic issues are involved. This is well illustrated in Europe, where the push to EMU among the members of the EU is clearly tied in with a desire for increased economic integration. Chapter 7 provided a framework for thinking about the interaction between two important OCA criteria, namely increased trade integration and correlations of real activity. Recent empirical work on Europe suggests that the relationship is generally positive. Increasing economic integration in Europe has been associated with higher correlations of real activity, making a single currency more attractive (although the size of this effect is less clear).[5]

These dynamics help to explain the relative stability of currency unions. If economic integration results in higher correlations of output, this can generate a self-reinforcing cycle in which economic integration encourages the formation of a monetary union, which in turn generates greater economic integration. To the extent that economic integration and monetary union also encourage political integration, this cycle is likely to be further reinforced by fiscal transfers from a centralized tax system, which will help to reduce idiosyncratic real disturbances. This process can help to explain why monetary unions are generally stable, and why, when they are dissolved, it is generally for political rather than economic reasons.[6] The observation that political boundaries generally coincide with monetary unions, therefore, does not imply that OCA theory is irrelevant for considering the value of proposed monetary unions.

Conclusions

What overall conclusions can be made about the interaction between financial integration and the real economy? Real behavior across countries appears to be different from that within them. This could reflect delays in adapting to the new environment of open capital markets. My own feeling, however, is that it is mainly a function of the barriers to financial integration inherent in separate currencies (at least in an environment of flexible exchange rates). Currency transactions are an attractive place to impose government regulations. Reversing the causation, the factors identified by OCA theory do seem to matter for currency unions. More speculatively, monetary unions appear to be self-reinforcing. Their existence encourages the dynamic changes which make them more attractive.

Together, these ideas point toward a world in which government will increasingly make choices between economic integration and monetary independence. In some cases, the choice will be toward increasing economic and monetary integration culminating in monetary union. This is exemplified by moves toward EMU in western Europe, a process which may well be repeated in other parts of the world. In others, preferences for monetary and political independence will tip the scales toward retaining floating exchange rates, even when economies are closely integrated. Good examples of this are the relationship between Canada and the United States, between Switzerland and Germany, and (assuming EMU goes ahead) between those who opt out of EMU and the rest of western Europe. Choosing appropriate levels of monetary and economic integration may become an increasingly important policy issue in the twenty-first century.

Notes

1 Implicit in this statement is an assumption that separate currencies tend to lower financial integration.
2 Particularly in the industrial world, where there are now virtually no controls on capital movements between countries. This contrasts with the situation even a decade ago, when many countries operated capital controls.
3 In addition to providing intertemporal trades, capital markets provide benefits such as insurance against unexpected disturbances. The tests using real variables therefore look at only one of the benefits emanating from open capital markets.
4 The following conclusions, from Goodhart (1995, p. 452), express some of these concerns: 'The evidence therefore suggests that the theory of optimum currency areas has relatively little predictive power. Virtually all independent sovereign states have separate currencies, and changes in sovereign states lead rapidly to accompanying adjustments in monetary autonomy. The boundaries of states rarely coincide exactly with optimum currency areas, and changes in boundaries causing changes in currency domains rarely reflect shifts in optimum currency areas.'
5 Frankel and Rose (1997) and Fatas (1997). However, Fatas also finds that while increasing European integration raises correlations between regions across European countries, it lowers correlations between regions within countries.
6 Political factors are, it should be noted, at the root of most economic policy initiatives.

Bibliography

For discussion and working papers the following abbreviations are used: CEPR, Centre for Economic Policy Research, London; IMF, International Monetary Fund, Washington, DC; NBER, National Bureau of Economic Research, Cambridge, MA; NIESR, National Institute for Economic and Social Research, London.

Alesina, Alberto and Vittorio Grilli (1992), 'The European Central Bank: Reshaping the Monetary Politics in Europe', in *Establishing a Central Bank: Issues in Europe and Lessons from the U.S.*, eds. Matthew B. Canzoneri, Vittorio Grilli and Paul R. Masson (Cambridge: Cambridge University Press).

—— and —— (1993), 'On the Feasibility of a One or Multi-Speed European Monetary Union', NBER Working Paper No. 4350.

——, Roberto Perotti and Enrico Spolaore (1995), 'Together or Separately? Issues on the Costs and Benefits of Political and Fiscal Unions', *European Economic Review*, Vol. 39, pp. 751–8.

—— and Lawrence Summers (1993), 'Central Bank Independence and Macroeconomic Performance', *Journal of Money, Credit and Banking*, Vol. 25, pp. 151–62.

Alogoskoufis, George and Ron Smith (1991), 'The Phillips Curve, the Persistence of Inflation and the Lucas Critique: Evidence from Exchange Rate Regimes', *American Economic Review*, Vol. 81, pp. 1254–75.

Anderton, Robert and Ray Barrell (1993), 'The ERM and Structural Change in European Labour Markets: A Study of 10 Countries', NIESR Discussion Paper No. 40.

Artis, Michael and Tamim Bayoumi (1990), 'Saving, Investment, Financial Integration and the Balance of Payments', *Staff Studies for the World Economic Outlook: September 1990* (Washington: International Monetary Fund).

Asdrubali, Pierfederico, Bent E. Sorensen and Oved Yosha (1996), 'Channels of Interstate Risksharing, U.S. 1963–90', *Quarterly Journal of Economics*, Vol. 111, pp. 1081–110.

Atkeson, Andrew and Tamim Bayoumi (1993), 'Do Private Capital Markets Insure Regional Risk? Evidence from the United States and Europe', *Open Economies Review*, Vol. 4, pp. 303–24.

Backus, David K., Patrick J. Kehoe and Finn E. Kyland (1992), 'International Real Business Cycles', *Journal of Political Economy,* Vol. 100, pp. 745–75.

Baldwin, Richard (1989), 'The Growth Effect of EMU', *Economic Policy*, Vol. 4, pp. 248–81.

Barro, Robert J. (1974), 'Are Government Bonds Net Wealth?', *Journal of Political Economy*, Vol. 82, pp. 1095–117.

Barro, Robert J. and David Gordon (1983), 'Rules, Discretion and Reputation in a Model of Monetary Policy', *Journal of Monetary Economics*, Vol. 12, pp. 101–21.

Baxter, Marianne and Mario J. Crucini (1993), 'Explaining Saving Investment Correlations', *American Economic Review*, Vol. 83, pp. 416–36.

—— and —— (1994), 'Business Cycles and the Asset Structure of Foreign Trade', NBER Working Paper No. 4975.

Bayoumi, Tamim (1990), 'Saving Investment Correlations: Immobile Capital, Government Policy or Endogenous Behavior', *IMF Staff Papers*, Vol. 37, pp. 360–87.

—— (1994), 'A Formal Model of Optimum Currency Areas', *IMF Staff Papers*, Vol. 41, pp. 537–54.

—— (1995), 'Explaining Consumption: A Simple Test of Alternative Hypotheses', CEPR Discussion Paper No. 1289.

—— and Barry Eichengreen (1993a), 'Shocking Aspects of European Monetary Unification', in *The Transition to Economic and Monetary Union in Europe*, eds. Francesco Giavazzi and Francisco Torres (Cambridge: Cambridge University Press).

—— and —— (1993b), 'Is There a Conflict Between EC Enlargement and European Monetary Unification?' *Greek Economic Review*, Vol. 15, pp. 131–54

—— and —— (1994a), 'Monetary and Exchange Rate Arrangements for NAFTA', *Journal of Development Economics*, Vol. 43, pp. 125–65.

—— and —— (1994b), *One Money or Many? On Analyzing the Prospects for Monetary Unification in Various Parts of the World*, Princeton Essays in International Finance No. 76 (Princeton, NJ: International Finance Section, Department of Economics, Princeton University).

—— and —— (1996), 'Operationalizing the Theory of Optimum Currency Areas', paper given at a CEPR conference, Regional Integration, held at La Coruña, Spain, 26–27 April.

—— and —— (1997), 'Optimum Currency Areas and Exchange Rate Volatility: Theory and Evidence Compared', in *Frontiers of International Economics*, ed. Benjamin Cohen (Cambridge: Cambridge University Press).

—— and Michael Klein (1995), 'A Provincial View of Capital Mobility', NBER Working Paper No. 5115.

—— and Ronald MacDonald (1995), 'Consumption, Income and International Capital Market Integration', *IMF Staff Papers*, Vol. 42, pp. 552–76.

—— and Paul R. Masson (1995), 'Fiscal Flows in the United States and Canada: Lessons for Monetary Union in Europe', *European Economic Review*, Vol. 39, pp. 253–74.

—— and —— (1996), 'Debt-Creating Versus Non-Debt Creating Stabilization Policies', unpublished manuscript, International Monetary Fund.

—— and Jonathan Ostry (1995), 'Macroeconomic Shocks and Trade Flows Within Africa: Implications for Optimum Currency Arrangements', IMF Working Paper No. WP/95/142 (also forthcoming in *Journal of African Economics*).

—— and Eswar Prasad (1995), 'Currency Unions, Economic Fluctuations and Adjustment: Some Empirical Evidence', CEPR Discussion Paper No. 1172.

—— and Andrew Rose (1993), 'Domestic Saving and Intra-National Capital Flows', *European Economic Review*, Vol. 37, pp. 1197–202.

—— and Gabriel Sterne (1993), 'Regional Trading Blocs, Mobile Capital and Exchange Rate Coordination', Bank of England Working Paper No. 12 (London: Bank of England).

—— and Alun Thomas (1995), 'Relative Prices and Economic Adjustment in the U.S. and EU: A Real Story About European Monetary Union', *IMF Staff Papers*, Vol. 42, pp. 108–33.

Bean, Charles (1992), 'The Economics of EMU', *Journal of Economic Perspectives*, Vol. 6, pp. 31–52.

Bernheim, B. Douglas (1987), 'Ricardian Equivalence: An Evaluation of Theory and Evidence', in *NBER Macroeconomics Manual 1987* (Cambridge, MA: MIT Press).

Bini-Smaghi, Lorenzo and Silvia Vori (1993), 'Rating the EC as an Optimal Currency Area', Temi di discussione del Servizio Studi, No. 1987, Banca d'Italia, January.

Blanchard, Olivier and Lawrence Katz (1992), 'Regional Evolutions', *Brookings Papers on Economic Activity 1992*, Vol. 1, pp. 1–75.

—— and Pierre Alain Muet (1993), 'Competitiveness Through Disinflation: An Assessment of the French Macroeconomic Strategy', *Economic Policy*, Vol. 16, pp. 11–56.

—— and Daniel Quah (1989), 'The Dynamic Effects of Aggregate Demand and Supply Disturbances', *American Economic Review*, Vol. 79, pp. 655–73.

Boadway, Robin W. and Paul A. R. Hobson (1993), 'Intergovernmental Fiscal Relations in Canada', *Canadian Tax Foundation Paper Number 96* (Toronto: Canadian Tax Foundation).

Borio, Claudio E. V. (1996), 'Credit Characteristics and Monetary Policy

Transmission Mechanisms in Fourteen Industrial Countries: Facts, Conjectures and Some Econometric Evidence', in *Monetary Policy in a Converging Europe,* eds. Koos Alders, Kees Koedijk, Clemens Kool and Carlo Winder (Dordrecht: Kluwer Academic Publishers).

Boughton, James M. (1993), 'The Economics of the CFA franc Zone', in *Policy Issues in the Operation of Currency Unions*, eds. Paul R. Masson and Mark P. Taylor (Cambridge: Cambridge University Press).

Browning, Martin and Annamaria Lusardi (1996), 'Household Saving: Micro Theories and Micro Facts', *Journal of Economic Literature*, Vol. 34, pp. 1797–855.

Buiter, Willem (1995), 'Macroeconomic Policy During the Transition to Monetary Union', CEPR Discussion Paper No. 1222.

Canova, Fabio and Morton O. Ravn (1994), 'International Consumption Risk Sharing', CEPR Discussion Paper No. 1074.

Canzoneri, Matthew B. and Carol Ann Rogers (1990), 'Is the European Community an Optimal Currency Area? Optimal Taxation Versus the Cost of Multiple Currencies', *American Economic Review*, Vol. 80, pp. 419–33.

Casella, Alessandra (1992), 'Voting on the Adoption Rules of a Common Currency', in *Establishing a Central Bank: Issues in Europe and Lessons from the U.S.*, eds. Matthew B. Canzoneri, Vittorio Grilli and Paul R. Masson (Cambridge: Cambridge University Press).

Chamie, Nick, Alain DeSerres and Rene Lalonde (1994), 'Optimum Currency Areas and Shock Asymmetry: A Comparison of Europe and the United States', Bank of Canada Working Paper No. 94–1 (Toronto: Bank of Canada).

Cohen, Daniel and Charles Wyplosz (1989), 'The European Monetary Union: An Agnostic Evaluation', in *Macroeconomic Policies in an Interdependent World*, eds. Ralph Bryant, David Currie, Jacob Frenkel, Paul Masson and Richard Portes (Washington, DC: International Monetary Fund).

Cole, Harold L. and Maurice Obstfeld (1991), 'Commodity Trade and International Risk Sharing: How Much Do Financial Markets Matter?' *Journal of Monetary Economics*, Vol. 28, 3–24.

Commission of the European Communities (1990), 'One Market, One Money: An Evaluation of the Potential Benefits and Costs of Forming an Economic and Monetary Union', *European Economy*, No. 44.

Corden, W. Max (1972), *Monetary Integration*, Essays in International Finance No. 93 (Princeton, NJ: International Finance Section, Department of Economics, Princeton University).

Corporale, Guglielmo Maria (1993), 'Is Europe an Optimum Currency Area? Symmetric Versus Asymmetric Shocks in the EC', *National Institute Economic Review*, Vol. 144, pp. 93–105.

Cumby, Robert E. and Frederick S. Mishkin (1986), 'The International Linkage of Real Interest Rates: The European–U.S. Connection', *Journal of International Money and Finance,* Vol. 5, pp. 5–23.

de Grauwe, Paul (1992), *The Economics of Monetary Integration* (Oxford: Oxford University Press).

—— and Wim Vanhaverbeke (1992), 'Is Europe an Optimum Currency Area?: Evidence from Regional Data', in *Policy Issues in the Operation of Currency Unions*, eds. Paul R. Masson and Mark P. Taylor (Cambridge: Cambridge University Press).

Decressin, Jörg and Antonio Fatas (1995), 'Regional Labour Market Dynamics in Europe', *European Economic Review*, Vol. 36, pp. 1627–55.

Delors Committee (1989), *Report on Economic and Monetary Union in the Economic Community*, Committee for the Study of Economic and Monetary Union (Brussels: Commission of the European Communities).

Dekle, Robert (1995), 'Saving–Investment Associations and Capital Mobility: On the Evidence from Japanese Regional Data', International Finance Discussion Paper No. 496, Board of Governors of the Federal Reserve System.

Dooley, Michael, Jeffrey Frankel and Donald J. Mathieson (1987), 'International Capital Mobility: What Do Saving Investment Correlations Tell Us?' *IMF Staff Papers*, Vol. 34, pp. 503–30.

Dowd, Kevin and David Greenway (1993), 'Network Competition, Network Externalities and Switching Costs: Towards an Alternative View of Optimum Currency Areas', *Economic Journal*, Vol. 103, pp. 1180–9.

Edison, Hali J. and B. Dianne Pauls (1993), 'A Re-Assessment of the Relationship Between Real Exchange Rates and Real Interest Rates: 1974–1990', *Journal of Monetary Economics*, Vol. 31, pp. 165–88.

Eichengreen, Barry (1990), 'One Money for Europe? Lessons from the United States Currency and Customs Union', *Economic Policy*, Vol. 10, pp. 117–87.

—— (1992a), 'Is Europe an Optimum Currency Area?', in *European Economic Integration: The View from Outside*, eds. Silvio Borner and Herbert Grubel (London, Macmillan).

—— (1992b), 'Labor Markets and European Monetary Unification', in *Policy Issues in the Operation of Currency Unions*, eds. Paul R. Masson and Mark P. Taylor (Cambridge: Cambridge University Press).

—— (1992c), *Is the Maastricht Treaty Worth Saving?*, Princeton Essays in International Finance No. 74 (Princeton, NJ: International Finance Section, Department of Economics, Princeton University).

—— (1993), 'Epilogue: Three Perspectives on the Bretton Woods System', in *A Retrospective on the Bretton Woods System*, eds. Michael D. Bordo and Barry Eichengreen (Chicago: University of Chicago Press).

—— (1995), *International Monetary Arrangements for the 21st Century* (Washington, DC: Brookings Institution).

Engel, Charles and John Rogers (1994), 'How Wide is the Border?', NBER Working Paper No. 4829.

Erkel-Rousse, Helene and Jacques Melitz (1995), 'New Empirical Evidence on the Costs of Monetary Union', CEPR Discussion Paper No. 1169.

Fatas, Antonio (1997), 'EMU: Countries or Regions? Lessons from the EMS Experience', *European Economic Review* (forthcoming).

Feldstein, Martin (1983), 'Domestic Saving and International Capital Movements in the Long Run and Short Run', *European Economic Review*, Vol. 21, pp. 129–51.

—— and Phillippe Bacchetta (1991), 'National Saving and International Investment', in *National Saving and Economic Performance*, eds. Douglas B. Bernheim and John B. Shoven (Chicago: Chicago University Press).

—— and Charles Horioka (1980), 'Domestic Saving and International Capital Flows', *Economic Journal,* Vol. 90, pp. 314–29.

Fieleke, Norman S. (1982), 'National Saving and International Investment', *Saving and Government Policy*, Federal Reserve Bank of Boston Conference Series No. 25 (Boston: Federal Reserve Bank of Boston).

Fishlow, Albert (1985), 'Lessons from the Past: Capital Markets during the Nineteenth Century and the Inter-War Period', *Industrial Organization*, Vol. 39, pp. 383–439.

Flemming, J. Marcus (1971), 'On Exchange Rate Unification', *Economic Journal*, Vol. 81, pp. 467–88.

Fogel, Robert William (1964), *Railroads and American Growth: Essays in Econometric History* (Baltimore: Johns Hopkins University Press).

Frankel, Jeffrey A. (1993), 'Quantifying Capital Mobility in the 1980s', in *On Exchange Rates* (Cambridge: MIT Press).

—— and Shang-Jin Wei (1993), 'Trade Blocs and Currency Blocs', NBER Working Paper No. 4335.

—— and Andrew Rose (1997), 'Is EMU More Justifiable *Ex Post* than *Ex Ante*?', *European Economic Review* (forthcoming).

Frenkel, Jacob A., Morris Goldstein and Paul R. Masson (1991), 'Characteristics of a Successful Exchange Rate System', IMF Occasional Paper No. 82.

Friedman, Milton (1953), 'The Case for Flexible Exchange Rates', in *Essays in Positive Economics* (Chicago: University of Chicago Press).

French, Kenneth R. and James M. Poterba (1991), 'Investor Diversification and International Equity Markets', *American Economic Review,* Vol. 81, pp. 222–6.

Froot, Kenneth A., Michael Kim and Kenneth Rogoff (1995), 'The Law of One Price Over 700 Years', NBER Working Paper No. 5132.

Fujita, Masahisa and Jacques-Francois Thisse (1996), 'The Economics of Agglomeration', CEPR Discussion Paper No. 1344.

Funke, Michael (1995), 'Europe's Monetary Future: One Market, One Money?' Humboldt-Universitat zu Berlin Discussion Paper Economics Series No. 38.

Gagnon, Joseph E. (1993), 'Exchange Rate Variability and the Level of International Trade', *Journal of International Economics*, Vol. 34, pp. 269–87.

—— and Mark D. Unferth (1993), 'Is there a World Interest Rate?' International Finance Discussion Papers No. 454, Board of Governors of the Federal Reserve System.

Ghosh, Atish R. (1995), 'International Capital Mobility Amongst the Major Industrialized Countries: Too Little or Too Much?' *Economic Journal*, Vol. 105, pp. 107–28.

—— and Jonathan D. Ostry (1992), 'Macroeconomic Uncertainty, Precautionary Saving and the Current Account', IMF Working Paper No. WP/92/72.

—— and Holger C. Wolf (1994), 'How Many Monies? A Genetic Approach to Finding Optimum Currency Areas', NBER Working Paper No. 4805.

—— and —— (1996), 'What Moves U.S. Business Cycles? Sectoral versus Geographic Shocks', paper given at the 1996 American Economic Association Meetings, San Francisco, 5–7 January.

Giavazzi, Francesco and Marco Pagano (1988), 'The Advantage of Tying One's Hands', *European Economic Review*, Vol. 32, pp. 1055–82.

Giovannini, Alberto (1993), 'Bretton Woods and its Precursors: Rules Versus Discretion in the History of International Monetary Regimes', in *A Retrospective on the Bretton Woods System*, eds. Michael Bordo and Barry Eichengreen (Chicago: University of Chicago Press).

Goldberg, Linda (1993), 'Exchange Rates and Investment in United States Industry', *Review of Economics and Statistics*, Vol. 75, pp. 575–88.

Goldstein, Morris, David Folkerts-Landau and others (1993), *International Capital Markets: Part II. Systemic Issues in International Finance*, World Economic and Financial Surveys (Washington, DC: International Monetary Fund).

Goodhart, Charles (1995), 'The Political Economy of Monetary Union', in *Understanding Interdependence: The Macroeconomics of the Open Economy*, ed. Peter B. Kenen (Princeton, NJ: Princeton University Press).

—— and Stephen Smith (1993), 'Stabilization', *European Economy* No. 5 1993, The Economics of Community Public Finance, Reports and Studies, pp. 417–55.

Grilli, Vittorio and Gian Maria Milesi-Ferretti (1995), 'Economic Effects and Structural Determinants of Capital Controls', *IMF Staff Papers*, Vol. 42, pp. 517–51.

Group of Ten (1993), *International Capital Movements and Foreign Exchange Markets: A Report to the Ministers and Governors of the Group of Deputies* (Rome: Bank of Italy).

Hall, Robert (1978), 'Stochastic Implications of the Life Cycle–Permanent Income Hypothesis: Theory and Evidence', *Journal of Political Economy*, Vol. 86, pp. 971–87.

Hallwood, Paul C., Ronald MacDonald and Ian W. Marsh (1996), 'Credibility and Fundamentals: Were the Classical and Interwar Gold Standards Well-Behaved Target Zones?', in *Modern Perspectives on the Gold Standard*, eds. Tamim Bayoumi, Barry Eichengreen and Mark Taylor (Cambridge: Cambridge University Press).

Helpman, Elhanan and Paul R. Krugman (1986), *Market Structure and Foreign Trade* (Cambridge: MIT Press).

Ingram, James C. (1962), *Regional Payments Mechanisms: The Case of Puerto Rico* (Chapell Hill: University of North Carolina Press).

International Monetary Fund (1984), 'Exchange Rate Volatility and the Level of International Trade', IMF Occasional Paper No. 28.

Irwin, Douglas (1996) 'The United States in a New Global Economy? A Century's Perspective', paper given at the 1996 American Economic Association Meetings, San Francisco, 5–7 January.

Ishiyama, Yoshihide (1975), 'The Theory of Optimum Currency Areas: A Survey', *IMF Staff Papers*, Vol. 22, pp. 344–83.

Jones, Matthew T. and Maurice Obstfeld (1994), 'Saving and Investment Under the Gold Standard', unpublished manuscript, University of California at Berkeley.

Kareken, John and Neil Wallace (1981), 'On the Indeterminacy of Equilibrium Exchange Rates', *Quarterly Journal of Economics*, Vol. 96, pp. 207–22.

Kempa, Bernd (1995), 'Monetary Shocks, Real Shocks and European Monetary Integration', Chapter 1 of an unpublished PhD thesis, *Real Shocks, The Real Exchange Rate and European Monetary Integration*, University of Toronto.

Kenen, Peter B. (1969), 'The Theory of Optimum Currency Areas: An Eclectic View', in *Monetary Problems of the International Economy*, eds. Robert A. Mundell and Alexander K. Swoboda (Chicago: University of Chicago Press).

Krugman, Paul R. (1980), 'Scale Economies, Product Differentiation and the Pattern of Trade', *American Economic Review*, Vol. 70, pp. 950–9.

—— (1991a), *Geography and Trade* (Leuven, Belgium: University of Leuven Press).

—— (1991b), 'Increasing Returns and Economic Geography', *Journal of Political Economy*, Vol. 99, pp. 483–99.

—— (1991c), 'Target Zones and Exchange Rate Dynamics', *Quarterly Journal of Economics*, Vol. 106, pp. 669–82.

—— (1993), 'Lessons of Massachusetts for EMU', in *Adjustment and Growth in the European Monetary Union*, eds. Francisco Torres and Francesco Giavazzi (Cambridge: Cambridge University Press).

—— and Antony J. Venables (1996), 'Integration, Specialization and Adjustment', *European Economic Review*, Vol. 40, pp. 959–67.

Kyland, Finn and Edward Prescott (1977), 'Rules Rather than Discretion and the Inconsistency of Optimal Plans', *Journal of Political Economy*, Vol. 85, pp. 473–92.

Lewis, Karen K. (1996a), 'What Can Explain the Apparent Lack of International Consumption Risk Sharing?', *Journal of Political Economy*, Vol. 104, pp. 267–96.

—— (1996b), 'Stocks, Consumption and the Gains from International Risk-Sharing', NBER Working Paper No. 5410.

Lucas, Robert E. (1978), 'Asset Prices in an Exchange Economy', *Econometrica*, Vol. 46, pp. 1429–45.

MacDougall, Donald (1977), *Report of the Study Group on the Role of Public Finance in European Integration*, collection of studies, Economic and Financial Series Nos. A12/B13 (Brussels: European Economic Community).

Mace, Barbara J. (1991), 'Full Insurance in the Presence of Aggregate Uncertainty', *Journal of Political Economy*, Vol. 99, pp. 928–56.

Masson, Paul R. and Steven Symansky (1992), 'Evaluating the EMS and EMU Using Stochastic Simulations: Some Issues', in *Macroeconomic Policy Coordination in Europe*, eds. Ray Barrell and John Whitley (London: Sage).

—— and Mark P. Taylor (1993), 'Currency Unions: A Survey of the Issues', in *Policy Issues in the Operation of Currency Unions*, eds. Paul R. Masson and Mark P. Taylor (Cambridge: Cambridge University Press).

McCallum, John (1995), 'National Borders Matter: Canada–U.S. Regional Trade Patterns', *American Economic Review*, Vol. 85, pp. 615–21.

McKinnon, Ronald I. (1963), 'Optimum Currency Areas', *American Economic Review*, Vol. 53, pp. 717–25.

Meese, Richard A. and Kenneth Rogoff (1983), 'Empirical Exchange Rate Models for the Seventies: Do They fit Out of Sample?', *Journal of International Economics*, Vol. 14, pp. 3–24.

Melitz, Jacques (1991), 'A Suggested Reformulation of the Theory of Optimal Currency Areas', CEPR Discussion Paper No. 590.

—— (1993), 'The Theory of Optimal Currency Areas, Trade Adjustment and Trade', CEPR Discussion Paper No. 847.

Messinger, Hans (1993), 'Interprovincial Trade Flows of Goods and Services', *Canadian Economic Observer*, Catalogue 11–010.

Mundell, Robert A. (1961), 'A Theory of Optimum Currency Areas', *American Economic Review*, Vol. 51, pp. 657–65.

Murphy, Robert G. (1984), 'Capital Mobility and the Relationship between Saving and Investment in OECD Countries', *Journal of International Money and Finance*, Vol. 3, pp. 327–42.

Mussa, Michael and Morris Goldstein (1993), 'The Integration of World Capital Markets', IMF Working Paper No. WP/93/95.

Mussa, Michael, Morris Goldstein, Peter Clark, Donald Mathieson and Tamim Bayoumi (1994), *Improving the International Monetary System—Constraints and Possibilities*, IMF Occasional Paper No. 116.

Norrbin, Stefan C. and Don E. Schlagenhauf (1988), 'An Inquiry into the Sources of Macroeconomic Fluctuations', *Journal of Monetary Economics*, Vol. 22, pp. 43–70.

—— and —— (1994), 'The Role of International Factors in the Business Cycle: A Multicountry Study', unpublished manuscript, Arizona State University.

Obstfeld, Maurice (1986), 'Capital Mobility in the World Economy: Theory and Measurement', *Carnegie–Rochester Conference Series on Public Policy*, Vol. 24, pp. 251–70.

—— (1992), 'International Risk Sharing and Capital Mobility: Another Look', *Journal of International Money and Finance*, Vol. 11, pp. 115–21.

—— (1994), 'Are Industrial Country Consumption Risks Globally Diversified?', in *Capital Mobility: Stabilizing or Volatizing*, eds. Leonardo Liederman and Assaf Razin (Cambridge: Cambridge University Press).

—— (1995), 'International Capital Mobility in the 1990s', in *Understanding Interdependence: The Macroeconomic of the Open Economy*, ed. Peter Kenen (Princeton, NJ: Princeton University Press).

—— and Kenneth Rogoff (1994), 'The Intertemporal Approach to the Current Account', NBER Working Paper No. 4893; also in *Handbook of International Economics*, eds. Gene Grossman and Kenneth Rogoff (Amsterdam: North Holland).

—— and —— (1996), *Foundations of International Macroeconomics* (Cambridge: MIT Press).

Poloz, Stephen (1990), 'Real Exchange Rate Adjustment Between Regions in a Common Currency Area', unpublished manuscript, Bank of Canada.

Poole, William (1970), 'The Optimal Choice of Monetary Policy Instruments in a Simple Stochastic Macroeconomic Model', *Quarterly Journal of Economics*, Vol. 84, 197–216.

Ricci, Luca A. (1996), 'A Model of Optimum Currency Areas', unpublished manuscript, Graduate Institute of International Studies Geneva.

Rogoff, Kenneth (1985), 'The Optimal Degree of Commitment to an Intermediate Monetary Target', *Quarterly Journal of Economics*, Vol. 100, pp. 1169–90.

Sachs, Jeffrey D. (1981), 'The Current Account and Macroeconomic Adjustment in the 1970s', *Brookings Papers on Economic Activity*, Vol. 1, pp. 201–68.

Sala-i-Martin, Xavier and Jeffrey Sachs (1992), 'Fiscal Federalism and Optimum Currency Areas: Evidence for Europe from the United States', in *Establishing a Central Bank: Issues in Europe and Lessons from the U.S.*, eds. Matthew Canzoneri, Vittorio Grilli and Paul R. Masson (Cambridge: Cambridge University Press), pp. 195–219.

Savvides, Andreas (1993), 'Pegging the Exchange Rate and the Choice of a Standard by LDCs', *Journal of Economic Development*, Vol. 18, pp. 107–25.

Sinn, Stefan (1992), 'Saving–Investment Correlations and Capital Mobility: On the Evidence from Annual Data', *Economic Journal*, Vol. 102, pp. 1162–70.

Stockman, Alan C. (1988), 'Sectoral and National Aggregate Disturbances to Industrial Output in Seven European Countries', *Journal of Monetary Economics*, Vol. 21, pp. 387–409.

Summers, Lawrence H. (1988), 'Tax Policy and International Competitiveness', in *International Aspects of Fiscal Policies*, ed. Jacob A. Frenkel (Chicago: University of Chicago Press).

Summers, Robert and Alan Heston (1991), 'The Penn World Tables (Mark 5): An Expanded Set of International Comparisons, 1950–88', *Quarterly Journal of Economics*, Vol. 106, pp. 327–68.

Tavlas, George (1993), 'The "New" Theory of Optimum Currency Areas', *The World Economy*, Vol. 16, pp. 663–85.

—— (1994), 'The Theory of Monetary Integration', *Open Economies Review*, Vol. 5, pp. 211–30.

Taylor, Alan M. (1994), 'Domestic Saving and International Capital Flows Reconsidered', NBER Working Paper No. 4892.

Taylor, Mark P. (1995), 'The Economics of Exchange Rates', *Journal of Economic Literature*, Vol. 33, pp. 13–47.

Tesar, Linda L. (1991), 'Saving, Investment and International Capital Flows', *Journal of International Economics*, Vol. 31, pp. 55–78.

—— (1995), 'Evaluating the Gains from International Risksharing', *Carnegie–Rochester Conference Series on Public Policy*, Vol. 42, pp. 95–143.

Thomas, Alun (1993), 'Saving, Investment and the Regional Current Account: An Analysis of Canadian, West German and British Regions', IMF Working Paper No. WP/93/62.

Tower, Edward and Thomas Willett (1976), *The Theory of Optimum Currency Areas and Exchange Rate Flexibility*, Special Papers in International Economics No. 11 (Princeton, NJ: International Finance Section, Department of Economics, Princeton University).

Ubide, Angel J. (1994), 'Is There Consumption Risk Sharing in the European Union?', European University Institute Working Paper No. 94/37.

van Wincoop, Eric (1994), 'Welfare Gains from International Risk Sharing', *Journal of Monetary Economics*, Vol. 34, pp. 175–200.

—— (1995), 'Regional Risksharing', *European Economic Review*, Vol. 39, pp. 1545–68.

von Hagen, Jürgen (1992), 'Fiscal Arrangements in a Monetary Union: Evidence from the U.S.', in *Fiscal Policy, Taxes and the Financial System in an Increasingly Integrated Europe*, eds. Don Fair and Christian de Boissieux (Deventer: Kluwer).

Weber, Axel (1990), 'EMU, Asymmetries and Adjustment Problems in the EMS: Some Empirical Evidence', CEPR Discussion Paper No. 448.

Wei, Shang-Jin (1996), 'How Stubborn are Nations to Global Integration',

paper presented at the 1996 American Economic Association Meetings in
San Francisco, 5–7 January.

Winkler, Bernhard (1995), 'Reputation for EMU: An Economic Defence of
the Maastricht Criteria', European University Institute Working Paper No.
ECO 95/18.

Index

Page references in *italics* refer to figures; those in **bold** refer to tables

Anglo-Saxon financial systems 110
Association of South-East Asian Nations (ASEAN) 1
automatic stabilizers 82–3

Baxter–Crucini model 35
Bretton Woods exchange rate system, collapse of 13

Canada
  consumption patterns 66–9, **67, 68**
  fiscal policy as automatic stabilizer 104–5
  saving–investment relationships 39–41, **40**, 42–3, **43**
  trade ratios 106–8, **107**
capital–labor ratio 34
capital mobility *see* international capital mobility
CFA franc zone 80, 89, 90
computational general equilibrium (CGE) models 112
consumption
  in Canada 66–9, **67, 68**
  effect of traded and nontraded goods on 64–5

effects of unemployment on 64–5
international patterns 66
see also risk sharing hypothesis
consumption smoothing 19–20, 54–5
see also risk sharing hypothesis
cross-sectional and time-series behavior, distinguishing between 37–8
currency union
  benefits of 111–13, 115
  break-up of 95
  disadvantages 1
  effectiveness of exchange rate 106–9
  evidence from large models 113–14
  nonmonetary response mechanisms 102–6
  policy conflicts 109–11
  stability 13
  underlying disturbances 96–102
  see also European Monetary Union; optimum currency areas

153

depression, great 12
devaluations 23
direct military intervention 25

economic integration 118–34
    impact on single currency
        operation 118–19
    optimum currency areas and
        129–32, 133
EFTA, underlying disturbances
    in 97–9
European Commission, trade
    integration 86, 118
European Monetary System 86
European Monetary Union
    (EMU) 1, 80, 89, 95, 96–
    101, 111, 138, 140
European Union (EU) 1
    economic disturbances 100–
    1
    Single Market program 11
exchange rate
    effectiveness in reducing
        economic disturbances
        85–7, 106–9
    industrial structure and
        86–7
    links with trade 111–12
    stability 47
    volatility 47, 111–12
Exchange Rate Mechanism
    (ERM) 1, 86, 97, 102
exchange rate peg 110
exchange rate regime
    fixed 81
    floating 132
    future of 14
    policies 78
exchange rate turmoil (Europe)
    (1992–93) 21

Feldstein–Horioka puzzle 2, 5,
    17–19, 30–3, 34, 41
    null hypothesis 35
    see also saving–investment
        correlations
financial deregulation 11
fiscal policy
    automatic stabilizers 104–5
    effect of 48, 82–3
    federal, impact on regional
        income 103
    institutional arrangements
        110–11
    transmission mechanisms
        109–10
future access to international
    capital markets 21

GDP as measure of real eco-
    nomic disturbances 97
German unification
    impact on EU currency union
        100
gold points 12
gunboat diplomacy 25

home ownership 110

income insurance 83, 84, 105
industry-specific disturbances 109
inflation, monetary policy and
    88–9
international business cycle 59,
    63–4
international capital mobility 1–
    3, 11–13
    consumption and 54–5
    saving–investment correla-
        tions and 30–2
    test results for 4–5, 13–25

International Monetary Fund
Articles of Agreement 12
intertemporal approach to the
balance of payments 55
intra-regional trade 106

Japan
deregulation of international
capital markets 11
offshore–onshore differential
16

labor and capital mobility 82,
84
as nonmonetary adjustment
mechanism 102–3
Latin American Free Trade
Association (LAFTA) 1
Lawson doctrine 49
liquidity constraints 19
Lucas 'coconuts' model 83
Lucas supply function 81

Maastricht Treaty 1, 95
mortgage loans 88, 110
Mundell on optimum currency
areas 78–9
Mundell–Flemming open
economy framework 81,
100

non-exchange rate adjustment
mechanisms 102–6
North America Free Trade
Agreement (NAFTA) 1
underlying disturbances in
99–100

Obstfeld 33–6, 38, 41
oil prices 82

onshore–offshore interest rate
differential 14–15, *16*
openness *see* trade
optimum currency areas 5–6,
138–40
benefits of 90–1
effectiveness of the exchange
rate 85–7
fiscal policies 82–3
income insurance 83, 84
industrial diversification 86–
7
labor and capital mobility 82,
84
Mundell on 78–9
nonmonetary mechanisms
81–4
policy conflicts 87–90
price rigidities 82
private capital markets 83,
105
underlying economic
disturbances 78, 79, 80–1,
96–101, **98, 99**
wage and price flexibility
81–2, 84
see also currency union
optimum tariff model 23–4, 26–
8
overlapping generations model
38

pre-1914 gold standard 2, 5, 12,
24–5, 35
cross-sectional saving–
investment correlation
during 43–4
precautionary saving motive 19
price flexibility 3, 81–2, 84
price rigidities 3, 82

private capital markets 83, 105
purchasing power parity (PPP)
    20
    deviation from 47
    failure of 15–17

real business cycle theory,
    international 3, 59,
    63–4
two-country model 35
real wage rigidity 102
regional disturbances 108–9
relative price rigidity 102
Ricardian effects 82
risk aversion 14
risk sharing hypothesis 5, 54
    consumption regression over
        OECD countries 60–3,
        61
    correlations of real GDP
        across OECD countries
        and 57–8, **58**
    empirical evidence 57–69
    failure of model of 63–4
    failure within countries 55
    labor–leisure trade-offs
        affecting 64
    model 55–7
    testing 59–60
    use of method of moment
        estimators 60
    use of vector autoregressions
        (VARs) 60

saving–investment correlations
    31–2, **32**
    across different time periods
        44–6, **44**, *45*
    Canada 39–41, **40**, 42–3,
        43

current account targeting 48–
    9
cyclical factors 37–8
in environments of high
    capital mobility 41–6
interpreting results 47–50
OECD countries
    (1960–93) 36–7, **36**, *37*
    (1961–86) 38–9, **39**
    private 42
    role of government policies
        48
saving–investment test 17–19,
    30–1
sectoral diversification 108
single currency *see* currency
    union
sovereign immunity 23
symmetry of expectations 14

tests of international capital
    mobility 4, 13, 134–7
    differences in results 20–4
    macroeconomic 17–20
    microeconomic 13–17
Thatcher government, abolition
    of capital controls by 11
time-series correlations 50
trade
    impact of increasing integra-
        tion on 129–32, 133
    integration, impact on
        disturbance 85–6, 106–8,
        118–19
    model of, between two
        industries 119–25
    openness to 106–7
transaction costs 24
two-country real business cycle
    model 35

two-industry model, role of
exchange rate within 125–
9

UK
flexible mortgage loans 88,
110
offshore–onshore differential
16
unemployment 64–5, 84

USA
fiscal policy as automatic
stabilizer 104–5
overvaluation of dollar 21

vector autoregressions (VARs)
60, 97, 100

wage and price flexibility 81–2,
84